C000224547

Praise

Secrets of the
Feel-Good Home

"Although why a home does (or doesn't) feel good defies definition, this book describes the principles – with concrete examples – so simply and clearly that anyone can create this feeling, even in an unpropitious building. This is an uncommonly sensitive, perceptive and insightful book."

—Christopher Day

Eco-architect. Pioneer of sustainable architecture and 'Consensus Design'. Author of 'Spirit & Place' and 'The Eco-Home Design Guide'.

"This is the book to get you out of your armchair. Throw away the magnolia paint and get beneath the skin of your home to reawaken the energy it wants to give you. Susan has opened the door, so take the next step."

—Raymond Catchpole
Chairman of The Feng Shui Society.

"Susan Swire's *Secrets of the Feel-Good Home* invites you into the splendid world of energy and how it can have a profound impact, not only on your home, but in the deepest sense how the energy of your living space can transform your life. This easily accessible book feels like a cozy seaside cottage beckoning you inside to have a pot of tea next to the fire, while watching the waves crash to the shore. Recommended."

—Denise Linn

Founder of the International Institute of Interior Alignment. Bestselling author of 'Sacred Space'.

"As the world looks increasingly harsh and so many places are in turmoil, having a quiet, calm space to soothe the soul becomes even more important. What Susan Swire has done so eloquently in this beautiful book is to set out the simple guidelines for you to arrange your home so that it provides a soothing and healthy container for your life. It's a great read full of practical tips. I found it inspiring and I'm sure you will too. It contains all the secrets and feng shui treasures that you need to help you get your home and life in order."

—Gina Lazenby

International seminar leader. Author of 'The Healthy Home'.

"Susan Swire has captured the very spirit of Feng Shui. She knows how to paint with words, filling every page of her book with evocative descriptions that guide you in seeing through your Feng Shui eyes and applying Feng Shui principles in your own home. She uplifts you while you learn, a most harmonious combination indeed!"

—Terah Kathryn Collins
Founder of the Western School of Feng Shui.
Bestselling author of the 'Western Guide to Feng Shui'.

"I like this book very much. It is straightforward, practical and inspiring. If you want immediately useful hints and strategies to make your home more open, spacious and attractive – even if you live in a small space – then Secrets of the Feel Good Home will be of great use to you. Highly recommended."

—William Bloom
One of Britain's leading educators in the field of contemporary spirituality and holistic development. Bestselling author of 'The Endorphin Effect' and 'The Power of Modern Spirituality'.

Secrets
of the
Feel-Good
Home

What works
& what doesn't

Susan Swire

First published in 2015 by Wordzworth Publishing
Second edition published in 2018

ISBN: 978-1-78324-106-4

The CIP catalogue record for this book is available from the British Library.

Where possible the materials for this book have been obtained from sustainable sources.

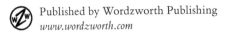 Published by Wordzworth Publishing
www.wordzworth.com

To Christopher Day MBE, eco-architect
You have given – and give – so much to the world

Acknowledgements

This is a book 'written by many' and I would like to thank you all. Some of you know who you are. Many don't. Thank you anyway.

Thank you especially to:

Peter, Doug and Kelly and the design team at *Wordzworth Publishing* who not only made this book possible but made it beautiful. *Peter, Doug and Kelly*, you could not have been kinder, more professional or more helpful. *Rhys*, you made the inside pages all I dreamt of but more than I ever thought possible. *Tom*, a big thank you for designing such a lovely book cover.

Those who have offered 'emergency' practical help along the way: *Cynthia & Andrew Colley* for giving your time and going out of your way one weekend to help. *John Taylor* for – only you know what – but I couldn't have managed without you.

Those of you helped me 'see' the world in a whole new way and without whom this book could never have been born:

Christopher Day for your inspiration, sublime architecture and friendship.

Denise Linn for your glorious and life-changing sunlit seminar on Feng Shui & Space Clearing (and much more) at the magical Shambhala Ranch in Northern California and the mega-watt love you showered on us all.

Terah Kathryn Collins for your amazing feng shui courses in San Diego, California. Never since has the world looked the same or been the same. You changed things for me forever and continue to do so.

And also to *Christopher Day, Denise Linn, Gina Lazenby, Raymond Catchpole, Terah Kathryn Collins and William Bloom* for endorsing this book. I feel honoured by your kind comments.

And to those friends who have influenced the text directly and indirectly, knowingly and unknowingly and/or whose homes have acted as inspiration ... including: *Alistair McKinnon, Cathy Doyle, Di Williams (Labyrinth), Irene & Paul Fowler (Quiet Garden), Ivy Collett, Jane Garland, Kathy Dixon, Kay Simon, Liz Bolton, Lynda Coney, Lynn Whyte, Melanie Reinhart,*

Nicola Waldron, Pat Burgin, Penny Hart-Woods, Peter Swire, Rita & John Bennett, Susan Beazley, Ursula Smilde-Hiatt. And a huge thank you to the many authors in the bibliography.

Thank you all.

About the author

Susan trained as a physiotherapist and dramatherapist in England and later in California as a feng shui consultant. The physiotherapy inspired an earlier book *Gentle Exercise*. The dramatherapy and feng shui, combined with a long-time passion for doing up houses, led to this one.

Her earliest memories are of an all-pervading 'sense of place' evoked both by the landscape and by the buildings around her. Dramatherapy and feng shui ignited this further; dramatherapy by revealing how, through the simplest of means, any space can be transformed into anything you want it to be and feng shui by demonstrating in precise but easy ways how any place, any home, can become truly a Home for your Soul.

She lives in the beautiful Yorkshire Dales National Park in the North of England. She works with clients, both individually and in small friendly informal groups, helping them harness the 'feel-good' within their own special places and spaces.

Contents

A Home for your Soul   1
    Home   3

Wellsprings   5
    Enchantment   7
    Inspirations   11
    Energy   15

Aspects of Harmony   17
    Location   19
    Placement   23
    Contrast   29
    Corners   37
    Flow   43
    Proportion   49
    Fractals   55
    Composition   65
    Ornament   69
    Simplicity & Abundance   73
    The Air We Breathe   83
    Space Magic   91

Dream Homes   103
    Threshold   105
    Door   111

Hall   117
Window   121
Ceiling   129
Staircase   137
Bedroom   143
Cubby Hole   153
Garage   157
Garden   161

Sanctuary   169
Fire   171
and to light your fire …   179
Blessing   181
Sacred Space   187

Feel–Good   195
The Big Six   197
The Dirty Dozen   199
Feel–Good   203

Appendix 1: Summaries   209
Feel–Good Secrets (Checklist)   211

Appendix 2: Shape Shifting   227
To Make a Space Feel Larger and Airier   229
To Make a Space Feel Cosier
and More Intimate   247
To 'Change the Shape' of a Room   253

Bibliography   261
References & Resources   263

And Now…   279
An Irish Blessing   281

We shape our home,
thereafter it shapes us.

Paraphrased from Winston Churchill
"We shape our buildings, thereafter they shape us."

A Home for your Soul

Home

What is home? What does it mean to us? What does it mean to you?

Maybe for most of us, most of the time, home is:

- ❧ Sanctuary
- ❧ Place of hospitality
- ❧ Operational centre for living

All that follows addresses one, two or all three of these factors.

As the operational hub the living space should be efficient, organised and contain only that which we love and/or use. Divide and rule is the key. A place for everything and everything in its place.

Giving and receiving hospitality is one of life's pleasures. For this, our home must be welcoming. It needs to be comfortable and beautiful and an expression of who we are, as idiosyncratic (or conventional) as we choose to be. Whatever our style, a *feeling* of abundance is the thing that makes it hospitable and inviting. This can mean having fruit, chocolate or flowers around or cups of hot tea readily offered or fresh home baking. Abundance does not mean extravagance. Abundance is a 'feel', a language, which can be simplicity itself. Abundance is warmth, a promise of comfort and acceptance. The most important person to feel welcomed, however, is you.

Above all home is sanctuary. It is our safe haven. It is calm and peaceful. Here we can relax and be who we are. This is where we are 'at home'.

Wellsprings

Enchantment

The sun is setting; luminous, gold, salmon, pink and flame amidst a few remaining flecks of tender blue, enough to make a sailor a pair of trousers as my grandmother used to say. There is a smell of farms, a good smell in those days. Memory reaches way back for some things. For me those early memories are saturated in the landscape. This is a place wild yet intimate with tiny buttercup fields carved from the moorland and long views of flat-topped hills. The rough-walled lanes, cobbled with stone setts, are edged with grassy banks, wildflower verges which soften the meeting of stone with stone. Today the walls remain but tarmac covers the setts and the verges are long gone to make way for traffic. At the time of my childhood things were different. The land was tinged with magic. Water sprites lived in the rocky streams. The little copse down the lane was an enchanted wood where the fairies danced at night. These places all had a 'feel'. Some were all-good with pools of sunlight, lovely to lie in. Some were dark and scary. I would be tempted there only to tear away in terror. In those days children's every move was not watched, monitored, shaped and guided as it is today. I ran free and drank of the mystery.

Very soon my attention turned to the few houses close by. The house on one side seemed beautiful and, as I revisit, I see that indeed it has 'perfect feng shui'. The house on the other side was inhabited by an ogre and woe betide when your ball fell over the wall into his shadowy ogre's den. Another house, a few steps away at the top of a dark steep narrow lane, held a deep and somewhat troubling fascination, both luring me and pushing me away. Our house was a haven mostly, although the wind howled in the attic and strange footsteps paced back and forth, back and forth.

This fascination with my surroundings grew into an obsession. By the age of three I knew that different places evoked different moods. Some made you feel protected and safe. Some exhilarated. Some were menacing. And so with houses. Each had its own aura, its own appeal. My godmother lived in a pretty doll's house and both she and the house nurtured me with love and safety. The rooms had windows on two sides and the light moved in magical ways, illuminating here, casting shadows there. Then all would change as another or another surface glimmered in the warm rays. The deep windowsills were the domain of coloured glass animals, living prisms of coloured light. And I was allowed to play with this magic menagerie.

At that time my friend Lynda lived in the tiniest cottage built into the hillside where the bilberries grew. Its floors were flagged with stone. Water from the spring flowed clear and cool into the stone sink and, by nightfall, flickering tendrils of gold light from the oil lamps glinted like will o' the wisps on the whitewashed walls. The fire in the hearth fired our hearts and stoked our imagination. Her mother's embroideries – quilts, cushions and pretty rag dolls, primitive art in reds and greens stitched with white – made this cottage glow and its simplicity and beauty has held sway over me ever since.

Sometimes I stayed overnight with friends and would lie awake wondering what I would do if this place were mine. What would I change? What's good here? What's not? And why? The why grew to haunt me and set me on a secret mission to discover what makes one place 'right' and another uncongenial, even disturbing. What, if any, are the constants that, universally, make us recognise a particular building or room or courtyard as beautiful through the ages, across cultures and regardless of climate, materials, style and underlying philosophy? If we could distil those qualities then maybe we could apply them to our own, often brutish, environment and make our world a more harmonious place. Especially it seemed important to discover how we could apply these laws, if they exist, to create magic in our home.

Such guidelines do exist. Not only do they exist but they are incredibly simple. At source they are intuitive. We 'know' them already as people everywhere always have. Additionally they have been analysed by visionaries ranging from the old feng shui masters to a few enlightened present-day architects, mathematicians and scientists. This is what these pages are about.

Inspirations

Taking inspiration from ancient and modern, East and West, our quest is for the eternal principles which can help us create the feel-good factor right here, right now.

The art of feng shui (pronounced fung shway) is thousands of years old but the aspects we explore here are bang up to date. They teach us about location and how to simulate a great location when we do not live in one right now. They explain how to sense and direct energy and work with light and shade for dramatic effect.

The old traditions of sacred geometry initiate us into the mysteries of pattern and proportion. Specifically we look at the Golden Mean or Divine Proportion and how we can apply it to create harmony in our home.

Fractal geometry has always been a feature of the built environment and is largely responsible for the vitality of our architectural heritage. Its use in former times, however, was entirely intuitive. It is only now that the computer has revealed the secrets of our fractal universe. Only now do we understand a little. Only now are we able to apply fractals consciously to enrich the places we inhabit. And only now are fractals conspicuous by their absence in most new building works (and we the poorer for it). In our context it means our spaces feel best when they are 'permeable' or 'fluid', link together as a coherent whole and have a rhythm which arises from repeating similar elements and subtle visual echoes.

We are deluged with ever-shifting design advice and are influenced and enriched by this. Fashion is fun. Here, in contrast, you will find many constants to use any place, any time, whatever the current mode, whatever your particular taste.

Empowered with a few simple secrets we can enliven the most beautiful or least promising of spaces from the tiniest to the grandest. If we combine these enduring precepts with our intuition we can all be alchemists and healers of our environment and create places of palpable peace and beauty. In turn our environment sustains us.

But remember if it feels right for you, it is right whatever the theory. Nobody knows the whole story and no one knows your story as intimately as you. Only you are familiar with the way the light falls in your home, how its layout serves you, what your needs and yearnings are and what is right for *you*. Go only with what you feel and what you love, using this book, as and when, as a guide. Above all, trust your intuition.

Energy

The following pages are all about optimising the feel-good factor in our home. Since the Chinese notion of 'ch'i' (pronounced chee) is such a brilliant tool in this context and, because we have no exact word for it, this book uses the term to represent 'energy', 'feel', 'atmosphere', 'aura', 'mood'. We will explore many ch'i-shaping secrets which make it easy to transform virtually any space into a vibrant delectable home. The premise is that everything is alive with ch'i, connected by ch'i and that ch'i is ever-changing. In the human realm it is easy to see how we impinge on others and they on us, how we are interconnected for better or worse and that change is the only constant. The inspiration of ch'i takes this much further. It shows that we are connected and in dynamic relationship with everything in our environment; with nature, our neighbourhood and our home because all are animated by the one energy. The ch'i of our possessions is seen as particularly potent since we endow them with personal associations and they 'speak to us' constantly. To accept that everything is alive, dynamic and interacting may mean suspending our judgement but, if we do, it transforms our relationship with the natural world, our possessions and each other.

Whilst energy is a single force, its clarity can be contaminated. Not all 'ch'i' sustains or makes us feel at ease. Sometimes it disturbs or even debilitates us. Some landscapes, buildings and maybe parts of our home are disquieting or discordant. We can, however, transmute energy that is less than sparkling.

Everything below is ultimately about harmonising ch'i to create that something special in our home.

Aspects of Harmony

Location

Location. Location. Location. If there is a choice between a better house or better location, which to choose? If you are looking for retail property which is the better move, great premises in a so-so location or a currently not-so-hot shop in a brilliant location?

Estate agents, universally, have no doubts. This has ever been so. Feng shui arose so many centuries ago because the rich and powerful desired the most auspicious locations for their large houses and small settlements. They employed those early seers, the first 'Land Form' feng shui masters, who observed the landscape as a wildlife photographer does today; listening and sensing, alert for signs and signals, vigilant, watchful. Instead of photographing wild nature for television they used the same intuitive skills borne of long practice, patience and experience to find the most vibrant places for nurturing life and community. The ideal location, we learn from them, is one that nestles safely below the winds (feng) of the high peaks and above the waters (shui) of the flood plains, between the wind and the water, the feng and the shui.

The perfect plot for these ancient landscape architects and maybe for us today, is one where the house and gardens are on the flat. The land in front slopes down to water (e.g. a river) and there is height (e.g. a hill) for protection behind. To a lesser degree the sides are protected likewise. A smaller front garden open to the view and a larger back garden shielded by a mountain, hillock, woodland or other raised protection offer 'prospect' (views/expansiveness) in front and 'refuge' (sanctuary/containment) behind. Feng shui dubs it 'mountain behind/open view in front'. This is the 'command position'. Think of it as the armchair location. The chair seat symbolises the plot of land, the back the high protection behind, the arms the lesser protection to the sides and the forward view the open aspect in front.

Lacking an ideal location, we can simulate one. Our 'mountain behind' may be invoked with trees, hedges, banks, walls, fences, summerhouses, hideaways or whatever fits the purpose. In front, space permitting, we can have a pond or fountain or simply a winding path suggestive of a stream. A grassy verge outside the front wall, maybe with flowers or a lavender hedge, feels expansive and generous. If the building fronts straight onto the road, window boxes, wall-hung flower baskets or leafy shrubs by the door can 'conjure up' the missing outlook.

Benevolent nature was pivotal to the feng shui siting of homes and settlements. Today we speak of 'well-heeled' leafy suburbs and 'down at heel' inner city districts. 'Well-heeled' and 'leafy' go together, the affluence and the leafiness (or their absence). These metaphors say a great deal. We gravitate instinctively to those places where there is an intimation of nature and invitation to wildlife. We can do much, however, to create our own Shangri-La even in the concrete jungle we may presently inhabit.

These insights about 'place' are as valid now as they were millennia ago. Our psychology is the same. The knife in the back is a universal fear. Have you ever walked alone at night, heart thudding, uneasy about the footsteps behind and gaining ground on you? We require, unconsciously, that sense of protection behind. We say: "Watch your back". Have you ever felt trapped when you could not see the way forward? We crave our vistas, physically and spiritually.

We rarely find the perfect location but can 'suggest' an armchair position wherever we are.

Placement

The one thing everyone knows about feng shui is that 'it has something to do with the way you arrange your furniture'. Yes it has. But this follows the rules of the 'command position'; protection behind, open outlook in front. We feel the effect of furniture placement every time we visit a restaurant, tea-shop or bar. Sitting at a table with your back to the wall means you settle down instantly and enjoy. You see what is going on. You are more interested (hopefully) in the person opposite but nevertheless you are able to scan the room even when not consciously aware of doing so. You know when your drinks are being brought to the table, when the food is on its way, who is coming through the door and who is sitting where. With your back exposed to the room you cannot quite relax in the same way.

The command position means we are always more comfortable with a wall or some substantial barrier behind plus a view of the door. This is the 'power spot' since, so placed, we feel empowered … and disempowered otherwise. The command position is the best place to sit, sleep and work and the best position for the principal piece of furniture in each room. It is rarely possible to place all the seating thus but we can compromise with high-backed chairs (or other protective screening behind) positioned to allow at least partial sight of the exit. To relax fully, we need to feel safe behind with a visible escape route ahead.

Two frequent culprits of the uncomfortable 'back exposed, no view of the door' position are kitchen work surfaces and home office desks. Ideally worktops face where people congregate and desks look into the room with a view of the door. Company chairmen always place their desks in this power position. A CEO never has his/her back to the room. Failing all else we can place mirrors to enable a view of the door and the room behind us.

Each space has a command position albeit with some flexibility. Whilst it is generally better to have a view of the door with your back protected, if (cynically) you are selling something, you may wish to give the client the chair with its back to the wall so they feel more comfortable and less on their guard. Or (more kindly) you may offer that seat to a friend who is feeling vulnerable in order to help them relax. Parents should have the power place, not the children and the boss, not the employees.

Any space is calmer and feels more spacious if its centre is empty. The centre is its point of balance. When I think of the harmony of a 'clear centre' I recall the tangible peace of cloisters within a tiny monastery on a Tuscan hilltop. I picture my friends' home in Southern California which has a minute but magical inner garden. I bring to mind the contained and sacred space of an ancient stone circle in the heart of England. Such perfect places all have open central space. Similarly one secret of a tranquil room is an empty centre. Where large rooms are zoned into smaller areas, each usually feels more peaceful with clear space at its core. We needn't be Spartan about it. A gorgeous rug can draw attention to and accentuate the empty space.

Think 'space between, behind and around'. Space between furniture promotes easy circulation. Space behind wall-hugging furniture makes a room feel lighter and airier, the effect being magically enhanced by concealed back-lighting. Space around everything, from the largest sofa to the smallest item, imparts maximum visual impact. With 'space around' even an apple takes on an iconic quality. The 'nothing touching rule' makes rooms 'bigger'.

Avoid too many cushions as this suggests that seating is 'spoken for'. I made a friend in the swimming pool and we often went back to her home. The obvious chair to sit on, the one I wanted to sit on, was out of bounds being occupied by a Victorian wax doll with big blue eyes and a straw hat. The doll sat in the inviting high-backed chair with the view of the door. She commanded the room. And "No." she said. "You are not sitting on my chair". Seating must look available if it is available. (If you have a precious chair with a wonky leg scheduled for the antique repairers, a big doll or beautiful cushion will deter anyone from sitting on it and potentially turning the chair leg and maybe their own into matchwood. Everything can work for, as well as against, you).

Many people buy furniture to set them up for life. They move to a larger or smaller house with different shapes of room and (at vast expense) cart their furniture around with them. What once looked great may do so no longer. One winter I 'cat sat' a friend's bungalow. Whilst in a wonderful rural setting the house was as architecturally uninspired as you can get. Crossing the threshold, however, you entered the most entrancing and harmonious interior. The owners had sold everything they owned along with their farm and big old farmhouse and started afresh. Each object had been acquired specifically and lovingly for the space, the corner, the wall where it now found itself. Each was beautiful and 'belonged' perfectly. There was not one surplus item, not an excess knife or fork. If a cup or saucer were broken they simply bought another. Yet everything needed was present. The whole was cosy, warm and aesthetically glorious.

For small spaces take a tip from the show home. You look around. This house is spacious. It is nice. It is very nice. But then, mysteriously, the same house inhabited has become decidedly poky. We must be mistaken. Maybe we are remembering the larger show home. No. We are learning a lesson. The illusion is simple. The designer downsized and created space. In a small area we should do the same. Keep everything in proportion. Get the scale right. In small rooms do not try and cram in too much. It is still possible to make a grand gesture with, say, a dramatic oversized painting or sofa providing everything else is in scale. As ever, with flair you can bend the rules. If big is what you really, really want but your space is miniscule, go for it but ensure the big is bold and beautiful with nothing superfluous to detract from it.

Notes

1. The essence of good location (outside) and placement (inside) is the same: 'Protection Behind' and 'View of the Way Ahead'. This is the 'command position' or 'power spot'.

2. Comfort and safety are paramount, so ensure all seating is ergonomically correct, comfortable and comfortable looking.

Contrast

Wishing to move from one area to another led to an extended house hunting spree. The brief was 'old cottage with character'. These don't come cheap anywhere and, craving unspoilt rural landscape, the search took place in a National Park. House after house, at exorbitant cost, was dark, poky and had oppressively low ceilings. Often they were stuffed with fusty furniture and weighted down with knick-knacks. Sometimes they smelt musty and dank. This was not the kind of character envisaged. These cottages were 'yin' in the extreme.

Extreme 'yang' is the opposite; minimalist, with large rooms, high ceilings, white expanses, big windows, very light, angular. Yang is sparsely furnished. It can be austere, stark, featureless. Or exciting.

The concept of yin and yang, the complementary aspects of ch'i, allows a subtle understanding of contrast and how to use it. Again, there being no exact translation, the terms are used as working tools. Things small, soft, dark and detailed are yin. Things light, bright, hard or large-scale are yang. We always feel more comfortable in places where contrasting qualities, yin and yang (rough and smooth etc.) are present. The yin-yang symbol, a circle of two interlocking sinuous halves like two fat tadpoles, expresses this succinctly. One tadpole is black but contains a white dot. Its twin is white with a black dot. The contrasting dots indicate our need for balance at all levels.

Contrast, a bit of both, is crucial to the vitality of our spaces. It was integral to all built environments until the 20th century. Now polarity is all but eliminated from our everyday architecture. When both yin and yang are there, each attribute has more impact than it has alone. Think of the dappled light and shade in woodland on a summer's day or the heightened reality evoked by sun and shadow in a beautifully shot film. Our homes and communities simply have more oomph when there is a harmonious balance of yin and yang as the one brings life to the other. Following is a yin-yang checklist for the home:

Yin (feminine)	Yang (masculine)
Back	Front
Black	White
'Cave'	'Clearing' *(Bibliography: Bangs)*
Contained	Expansive
Cosy	Minimalist
Curving	Straight
Dark, subdued	Light, bright
Delicate	Bold
Enclosed, secluded	Exposed, wide open
Floral	Geometric
Fragile	Robust
Heavy	Light
Horizontal	Vertical
Intimate	Grand
Low	High
Matt	Reflective
Meandering	Straight, direct
Narrow	Wide
Opaque	Transparent, translucent
Opulent, ornate	Simple, minimalist
Patterned, fancy	Plain, blank canvas
Private	Public
Refuge	Prospect
Restful	Stimulating
Rounded	Angular, sharp, pointed
Rough, fluffy	Smooth
'Sanctuary'	'Steeple' *(Bibliography: Lawlor)*
Shade	Light, sunlight
Short, small	Tall, large, big
Soft	Hard

Mini lists are possible as here for lighting:

Yin	Yang
Down lighting	Up lighting
Soft lighting	Strong lighting
Dimly lit	Brightly lit
Fairy lights	Flood lights

In home décor horizontal stripes are yin, vertical stripes yang; floral prints are yin, plain fabrics yang; soft gauzy curtains yin, un-patterned flat blinds yang; dark colours yin, pale and bright colours yang. Squishy overstuffed upholstery is yin, angular furniture yang; overabundance yin and chalk-white minimalism yang. In practice yin and yang, shade and light, are part of a continuum. Brown is yin compared to beige. Beige is yin compared to cream. Cream is yin compared to white but yang compared to beige.

Should a space feel too yang and comfortless you can bring in more yin and/or reduce the yang. If claustrophobic or cloying or in any way overly yin, reduce yin and/or increase yang. Do it your way. The options are endless. Soft (yin) tactile fabrics are the simplest quick fix for any too-yang space. Alternatively in an energy-draining excessively yin room you could use lashings of white and replace lots of little (yin) pictures with one large, strong (yang) painting or leave walls clear. A touch of black, unexpectedly, increases the sense of space – and adds pizzazz. Balance can be achieved by ranging freely through the lists. Other than with light and shade it is unnecessary to match each quality directly with its own polar opposite.

Whilst balance is crucial for comfort, some of us feel more secure in surroundings that veer to the yin and others more liberated with a little extra yang and we can make allowances for this. Different rooms too require some weighting. Bedrooms should be restful and yin, social areas more yang. If doing a temporary makeover for a party we might make it very seductive, dark, mysterious, yin. If in our home office we have to focus on analytical matters we can lean towards the yang with a large desk, plain walls and clear light. Providing both yin and yang are present, the precise balance is up to you. Best is to follow your intuition and then, if you wish, use the lists above to refine your choices.

Some (a very few) things simultaneously impart vitality (yang) and tranquillity (yin) as for example; flowers, cut-glass crystals and candles. A fire crackling in the hearth makes any room feel more alive (yang) and cosier (yin).

By the simplest of means you can enrich your home with emotional light and shade and make it a haven of subtle beauty. Everyone will wonder how you did it. They will conclude you were lucky to find such a nice house. But, once initiated into the mysteries of yin and yang, you know you can make almost anywhere a wondrous place to be.

Deep down, yin is our inner world – the unseen; our thoughts, beliefs, desires, dreams and aspirations. Yang is the outer world – the seen; the physical, our place in the world, our shared reality. We need to bring yin to our yang and yang to our yin. We do this by going deep within and taking our insights and treasure back into the world out there and making it the most beautiful we can (and using that to further enrich our inner world).

Notes

1. We 'like' rounded shapes more than angular ones. Sharpness activates the amygdala (fear-processing area of the brain) but is perceived as more interesting and thought-provoking. (*Bibliography: Bar et al. Lidwell et al*) For yin/yang harmony, use both but with discrimination. For overall comfort, safety, nurturing, beauty and pleasing first impressions, go rounded. Angular or pointed objects are useful for focussing attention.

2. Yin and yang *are* somewhat enigmatic. Whilst we work with them individually as above, these twin manifestations of ch'i are actually one with the other.

Perhaps the 'chiaroscuro' (bright-dark) technique of art and film comes closest to expressing this.

Caution

Although undoubtedly verticals make a space feel higher, strong verticals as in striped wallpapers and vertical blinds can have an unsettling effect at some deep level. This is seen in another context in the business-executive fashion for pin stripes … to self-empower (by disempowering you). Generally it is better to avoid regular, definite, repetitive verticals in our rooms in favour of soft upward-growing plants, vertical art and tall wall hangings etc.

Corners

Desert tribes, it is said, have countless words for sand and Arctic peoples an equally impressive number for snow. Is it not extraordinary then that we who live in such an angular world have but one word for corner? There are two categories of corner, the concave (inner/internal) corner as in the four corners of a room and the convex (outer/external or 'jutty-out') corner or 'arris'. Each has its subgroups; the right angles, the angles of less than 90° and the angles of more than 90°. There are the sharp corners that appear as cut with some sort of precision instrument. There are the rounded corners. There are those on some older buildings that are so round they barely qualify for our sole word 'corner'. There are corners that are square, still 'firm' but somewhat softened. There are many qualities and combinations of corner.

We disregard corners and edges though the mood they engender is huge. We feel more at ease when corners are somewhat softened and, at some elemental level, we find sharp corners disturbing. Feng shui aptly names strongly defined inner corners 'cobweb traps' and sharp projecting corners 'poison arrows'. Contemporary design is characterised by its clean-cut corners and razor-like angles and these have a profound effect. They activate us. In a large shopping complex they urge us to buy. They have a must-have-now, must-do-now quality. Poison arrows are 'cool', contemporary, exciting – and aggressive. At home, however, knife-sharp angles are over stimulating. Importantly, by defining the limits of a room so clearly, they make the space feel smaller. Softer corners blur boundaries and rooms seem more spacious.

The 'cobweb trap' is the strongly defined inner corner found at the meetings of walls and ceilings, walls and floors and particularly of walls with walls. As the spider lures the fly to its web, harsh internal corners 'suck in' the vitality of the room and deaden the atmosphere. You can demonstrate this with sound. Clap your hands close to the surfaces of walls and in the centres of rooms or ring a bell or beat a drum. The more resonant the tone, the clearer the energy. Then clap in the corners. Often when the sound is clear elsewhere, in corners it is duller, more thudding, indicating stale stuck energy. Subliminally we register such corners as unpleasant. We never like to be 'cornered'.

'Poison arrows' are the destructive energy or 'cutting ch'i' emitted from sharp outer corners. There is more than one prestigious multinational building worldwide designed deliberately with exaggeratedly pointed façades in order to launch a permanent 'attack' on competitors. Not for nothing is this destructive energy also called 'killing ch'i'. Certainly much of the disquieting feel of many newbuild institutions such as hospitals results from their multiple, multi-directional poison arrows. Ever wondered why you feel edgy in these hard-edged places?

Poison arrows around the door push people away. Friends do not feel so welcome. Homecoming is not quite such a joy. Positive energy does not enter your home so readily.

Many things fire poison arrows at our heart; sharp-edged furniture, kitchen worktops, shelves, girders, the blades of Venetian blinds. Take care not to sit, stand, iron, entertain or watch television for prolonged periods or sleep where there is a sharp angle pointing towards you. Energetically, physically and visually a poison arrow is an agitating influence. An odd corner for an odd time won't harm but feng shui claims that persistent exposure to a line of cutting ch'i may impact poorly on health. The first requirement of comfortable environments is that they are and *feel* safe. Avoid sharp-edged furniture as it is energetically cruel and physically dangerous (and nowhere more so than in the bedroom where you may be drowsy and less alert). No wonder we speak of cutting edge design. 'Babyproof' your home for adults as well as infants.

Plastering determines ambience. Today we seal our spaces with a cold, hard, unforgiving gypsum-based render. The 'perfect' plastering job is one where the flat surfaces are plastic-smooth and the corners and edges are as clean-cut as if machine tooled. The plasterer is trained for years to achieve this. And it is highly skilled. But we are left with a box to live in, replete with hostile corners and devoid of atmosphere. With old buildings especially, such plastering is a travesty. There are the barn conversions, fantastic until you step inside to discover the place may as well have been built yesterday off a production line, all matt-flat and squared off. Then we have the old cottages expensively 'done up' but rendered with soulless insensitivity. Worst is the so-called dry lining, the cardboard parody of a plastering job palmed off on us by developers who simply attach plasterboard panels to the breeze block and skim over. The walls sound hollow and insubstantial. You cannot hang anything heavy on them. There is no sense of comfort. And these houses cost big money. Nor is this confined to new property. I had personal experience of this slipshod way of fake plastering in an unsympathetically renovated old cottage. It smelt yeasty, beery, boozy. It was only when its awful dry lining was removed that the mystery revealed itself. Something nasty was festering behind the boards and seeping through.

It is the plastering, especially over corners, which determines whether the rooms we inhabit form beautiful organic nurturing shapes or whether they are mere people-storage units. This is not to advocate rough plaster or suggest that every corner should be round but there is much to be said for subtlety and contrast, with some corners gently rounded and others firm; 'squarish' but soft. Traditional lime and clay plasters are still the most beautiful and healthy. Both allow buildings to breathe, regulate moisture and have a whole range of ecological benefits to commend them over most modern renders.

Vernacular buildings everywhere, built by local craftsmen intuitively honouring local materials, have always had somewhat softened corners. The uncomfortable 'knife edge' is a new phenomenon. It may do for the showcase department store. It is too prickly altogether for homes, schools and workplaces. For clinics and doctors' surgeries it is the reverse of healing.

We need to 'disappear' cruel corners. Lighting is the easiest quick fix since it causes a 'white out' of the harsh angles. Try up lighting in the (yin) inner corners and down lighting over the (yang) arrises. Horizontals or squares (e.g. boards or tiles) help mask sharp inner corners. Greenery in, over or along corners, edges and ledges softens them. The Art Deco method was to insert rounded mouldings vertically along the corners prior to plastering. These are still available and can be transformative. More radically, corners can be chamfered and re-plastered.

It must be stressed that there is nothing wrong with square corners and straight lines. Most corners are right angles by definition. 'Straight' is fine. The sterile, unsettling feel comes from the exaggerated blade-like angles and edges so prevalent today. Being surrounded by them has the effect of keeping your brain on high alert.

When buildings form beautiful shapes there is far less need for excess ornamentation. For calm spaces we need softened corners. The wonder is that gentle corners and soft plastering, the norm for millennia, look as marvellous in new houses where, magically, they take on a contemporary feel.

Flow

Everything must flow; feelings, fluids, finances. The flow needs to be balanced, gentle, continuous and reciprocal. Otherwise its torrents overwhelm us or stagnation causes blockages in our lives.

'Flow' in buildings flows from the main entrance to other doors and windows. To 'see' its pathways, stand at your front door. The other visible doors and windows indicate the main flows in the building. In the same way each room has its flow, discernible from its doorway. Though largely determined by the layout of the building, it is usually easy to override existing energy paths. By highlighting with sunlight or lamplight or pleasing eye-catching items we can direct the flow at will. 'Where the eye goes, energy flows'.

The flow is too fast (and we tend to feel restless) where doors and/or windows are directly opposite each other. The energy (ch'i) rushes straight from one and out the other leaving no sense of comfort in the intervening space. The larger the doors and windows, the faster the flow. When front and back doors face one another, the energy shoots straight through without nourishing those important places where everyone, including you, enters and leaves your home. Like wind tunnels, long narrow halls and passages act as conduits of ch'i which force the energy along too quickly, particularly when there is a door or window at both ends. The ch'i needs to linger and, as it were, bless each part of our home before moving on. Similarly when windows face each other, the life-enhancing light from one is pulled through the other and dissipated. It does not play on the walls or illuminate the room quite as it should.

Slow the flow through these spaces in any way possible. Furniture, open shelving, translucent screens, large plants etc. can act as traffic calming ('flow calming') measures when placed between a door and/or window which are directly opposite one another.

At other times the flow is too slow and leaves us feeling listless. Many workplaces, vast edifices built to impress, necessitate constant artificial ventilation and lighting, both key aspects of the 'sick building syndrome'. Energy is depleted. Workers can feel lacklustre and devoid of imagination. Air conditioning and slick décor change nothing. Yet these are the places where people are under pressure to perform. Homes too can have windowless rooms as in some bathrooms. Poky rooms, dark corners and unused spaces are all potential dams of congested ch'i leaving us feeling heavy, dull and lethargic. (A space that even looks too tight *is* too tight, possibly affecting resale if a potential purchaser wants to bring in solid, bulky furniture but misperceives it to be impossible).

The priority here is to open out claustrophobic areas and free-up the circulation. Having less stuff is often a start. The first objective is to clear clutter. Furniture and other items impeding flow can be repositioned and/ or reduced in quantity. Doors, stairs and passageways need to be wide enough. Flow is better when doors open into a room, not towards a wall as in Victorian houses and may be improved by keeping doors open. Sometimes we attract more light and improve the flow when we remove a door altogether (perhaps adding a curtain for winter evening cosiness).

Ch'i or life force is more active at the front of the house and quieter at the back so 'busy' (yang) rooms are better situated at the front and private, intimate (yin) areas at the back. Kitchens, home offices and living rooms are well placed at the front. Bedrooms, dining rooms and the places where we like to relax or just 'be' are better at the back away from street action and traffic. The reverse is often what we find when buying a house and many new houses are constructed back-to-front from this perspective. To compensate, we can change the rooms around or bring yin influences to the too-awake front bedrooms to quieten them and yang influences to rear home offices so we feel less dreamy and more in the mood for work.

Most important of all is the circulation around the building. Comfortable flow means unfettered space, enough for at least two people to walk side by side around the property. For a detached house this implies open access or a gate at both sides between front and back and not just at one side with a blocked up wall at the other. Given a choice between added space inside and space around, the free flow around always feels more congenial. Think of the 'space around' as the ch'i membrane which nourishes your home. If blocked or cluttered it does the reverse.

And nothing is forever fixed. One of the most exciting rooms in one of the most exciting houses I know is a large kitchen with virtually no natural daylight. Two friends, let's call them James and John, entertain in this cosiest and most dramatic of kitchens serving amazing food, risqué conversation and fantastic loving hospitality. They have turned a nightmare of an inner room into the most theatrical but warm and welcoming Aladdin's cave imaginable. Their magic is wrought by the juxtaposition of antiques precious and quirky, vibrant colour and mirrors reflecting the ever-present

candlelight, flickering fire and bottles of wine, all con-
spiring to make you totally at ease. They have expressed
themselves in their own wonderful way, transforming
an impossible room into pure delight.

We can do the same in *our* way in our impossible spaces.

Proportion

riends of mine bought a sweet little house. Very soon they decided to extend it. The new enlarged room was so beautiful and its proportions so pleasing that I had them measure it. It was 26ft by fractionally over 16ft (approximately 8m x 5m). I didn't know it then but this is pure Golden Mean.

Several harmonious proportions are found universally in old buildings. The best known is the golden mean. The golden mean has many names; the 'Golden Section', 'Golden Ratio', 'Golden Proportion', 'Divine Proportion', 'Phi Proportion' ('Phi' being the first letter of Phideas, sculptor in chief of the Parthenon in ancient Athens). This ratio is so ubiquitous in nature and complex mathematically that it has fascinated philosophers for centuries. Sunflowers, snowflakes, eggs, apple blossom, seashells, the branching of trees, all accord to the golden proportion in which the shorter dimension is roughly 62% (or 5/8) of the longer. The exact ratio is 1:1.618 or, more accurately still, 1:1.6180339887499 ... forever. You never quite get there. For easy visualisation think of a credit card which is roughly golden mean, width to length, a 'golden rectangle, a 'perfect' shape (especially when there is plenty of credit on it).

The human form has multiple golden mean proportions. The ratio of the distance between the feet to the navel to the overall height is 1.618, or the golden mean. The 'lub dub' of our heartbeat is golden mean. The lub is 1 to the dub's 1.618. The average width of our mouth is 1.61 greater than the width of our nose. Plastic surgeons use this ratio for facial reconstruction.

The golden mean governs many growth patterns in nature. The nautilus shell is an oft-quoted example. The shell is a spiral of separate chambers which, together, take the golden mean proportion. Each chamber spirals around the previous one, increasing in size from the innermost to the outermost, each in the ratio of 1:1.618. As the nautilus grows and new chambers are added, the proportion and overall shape are maintained.

The golden proportion characterises much great art whether our taste is for the Mona Lisa, Monet or Mondrian. It is present in music from Bach to Britney.

We instinctively recognise the harmony of a building, room or window when it concurs with the golden mean. Many Georgian buildings demonstrate the 1:1.618 ratio throughout. Chartres Cathedral in France, the San Marco Church in Venice, aspects of the Great Pyramid in Egypt are a few legendary buildings displaying golden mean proportioning. We resonate with the harmony because we know it from our own structure and from the natural world about us. Even babies respond positively to it.

Of all proportions the golden mean is regarded as the most pleasing to the eye and we can make great practical use of it for bringing harmony and beauty to our home. You do not have to be precise (nature is rarely so). You only need introduce some approximation of it to transform a space.

There are simple ways of doing this. One way is playing with numbers. There is a number sequence which approximates the golden mean. Here is how it goes: 2+3=5; 3+5=8; 5+8=13. By continuing to add the two adjacent numbers in the sequence you arrive at a string of numbers which pans out like this: 1, 2, 3, 5, 8, 13, 21, 34, 55 and on forever. Take any two consecutive numbers in the series (over 3) and you have, near enough, the golden mean. If you wish to introduce an item of golden ratio to help balance a poorly proportioned space, you could, for instance, add a rug or table or mirror of perhaps 34in × 55in (about 86.4cm × 140cm).

In practice the 5:8 measure is generally used as the rough calculation for the golden mean. This means that (for example tripling the 5:8) a width of 15ft and length of 24ft (around 4.5m × 7.3m) feels good. If the room is too long and has an unsettling tunnel-like feel it can be calmed instantly by 'shortening' it, say with a sofa or chest of drawers placed at a point which leaves one end approximately in the 5:8 proportion. Though rarely appreciating why, everyone feels more at ease. All that is needed is a suggestion of the golden mean, not a rigid demarcation.

2, 3, 5, 8, 13, 21, 34, 55 (ad infinitum) are the Fibonacci numbers straight from sacred geometry. Fibonacci sequence applications are endless but, simple though it seems today, in times gone by this was a secret cipher available only to the greatest minds. Now we too, like those visionaries of old, can use it to create harmony.

There is yet another way which gives an exact result, one favoured by Renaissance artists and sculptors in planning their compositions before they ever lifted a brush or chisel. They used a simple tool known as a golden mean divider or calliper. Michael Schneider (Bibliography) describes how to make a divider which will find the golden mean point on a plan automatically without having to do any calculations whatsoever. You don't have to be a skilled carpenter or metalworker. You can use cardboard or drinking straws. It is as easy as that. If you are building or converting, it will help you design perfectly proportioned spaces from scratch.

One intriguing aspect of the golden mean is that if you take a square from a golden rectangle you are left with a smaller golden rectangle. Try it. Draw a rectangle of 5 x 8. Square it off inside. Within the original rectangle there is now a square and a smaller golden rectangle. Do the same with the smaller rectangle and you get the same result, ad infinitum. This can be useful in the cosying up of huge rooms or the laying out of large gardens.

The golden mean can be used for anything. Examples in our context are room shapes, garden areas, rugs, pictures, window frames, fireplace surrounds, mirrors, tables, small objects and the spacing between.

Albert Einstein said the golden mean: "… is a scale of proportions which makes the bad difficult *[to produce]* and the good easy". It certainly works wonders in bringing harmony to an unsettling room.

Fractals

Our homes and neighbourhoods are richer when they emulate fractal nature. But first we need to understand a little about the nature of fractals.

Swirling whirling twirling, on and on, the computer offers endless fascinating fractal images to play with, to download and the software to generate our own. This comes with a warning; don't – unless you want to get hooked.

Maybe the fascination is because we ourselves our fractal beings living in a fractal universe. Today as I walk home in the opalescent blue-pink before twilight, the trees in this country lane are about to burst into leaf. Their silhouettes, fractal-like, are all fluffy and 'fractured' against the sky. And fractal-like, the trunk branches into branches which branch into smaller branches and into still smaller branches, each connected to the whole. I return home and pick up one of my treasures, a small yew branch fallen from the oldest living thing in Britain according to the friend who gave it to me. My little branch branches into very little branches and in its branching repeats the forms of the trees I have just seen, the fractal pattern of trees.

There are no straight lines or smooth flat surfaces in nature. Nature is raw and strong and rough around the edges and when we open ourselves to it we are always astounded. We never become habituated, never bored. Nature is always new. And we find solace there.

Although perhaps the blueprint for the cosmos itself, fractals were only identified in the late 20th century, the term 'fractal' being coined in 1976 by Benoit Mandelbrot, the Polish-born mathematician and pioneer of chaos theory. Fractals have three characteristics: uneven edges (permeability), repetition at all levels of magnification (self-similarity) and connectedness between all their parts (linkage).

Firstly, their edges are either broken or continuous. If broken they are, as it were, 'perforated' and if continuous, they are 'indented' or 'convoluted'. Either way, their boundaries are 'permeable', that is never straight nor smooth.

Secondly, each larger part of the whole is self-similar to the smaller part, as the trunk to the twig. They repeat themselves at ever-decreasing scales. Visualise two mirrors placed opposite each other. An image is reflected forever, each image self-similar to but smaller than the one it reflects. Fractals are something like this. In the 'regular fractals' of geometry, the ones we can download, the amazing thing about them according to Mandelbrot is: "… that they are equally complex at any magnification". He says: "If you took a fractal and magnified it by 500x, you would see the same level of detail as you did on the entire thing … fractals are among the most beautiful of all mathematical forms". Self-similarity does not imply that a smaller element is identical to the larger but is, as the term suggests, 'similar'.

Thirdly, each element is connected, as the roots to the leaves. Every component, however seemingly random, is linked with all the others to form profoundly interconnected organised wholes.

The irregular, chance, chaotic patterns of nature are in fact highly ordered in ways that, prior to the computer, it was impossible to detect. Nature is fractal; undulating, self-reflecting and connected. Trees, the coastline of Britain, tributary-fed rivers, clouds, seashells, feathers, mountains, rocks, snowflakes, the veining of leaves, torrents of water, galaxies – all echo with fractal self-similarity. In nature the best known is the fern because its self-similarity is so apparent. The fern is made up of fern leaves which consist of mini fern leaves and those again of micro ferns. A fern is a fractal universe in itself. Or take a cauliflower. It is a certain shape and size with an uneven 'fractured' surface. It consists of florets. We can think of each floret as a tiny cauliflower consisting of even smaller floret-caulis. Each floret is convoluted, self-similar and linked to the cauliflower in its entirety. This is fractal nature. We too are fractal-like, as in our limbs and veins and nervous system. Fractals occur at microscopic scales right down to our every DNA molecule. At macro levels the universe itself appears to be fractal.

Sometimes fractals are described by their dynamic properties: 'Fractals are the unique, irregular patterns left behind by the unpredictable movements of the chaotic world at work' as in the weather, water spiralling from a tap, the dance of autumn leaves tumbling to the ground, animal migrations, even the stock market. In the outwardly haphazard there is fractal order. Fractal geometry helps predict the previously unpredictable, with ever-increasing applications in science and technology.

Maybe even more astounding is the fractal-like nature of so much of the sacred and vernacular architecture worldwide, coupled with the almost complete dearth of fractal properties in much contemporary construction. Buildings are not pure fractals of course.

They are not self-similar across all their scales but their fractal properties over certain ranges of scale impart an integrity with which we resonate.

The Parthenon in Athens is a classical example of fractal architecture with its self-similarity, its perforations and its 'wholeness'. Aspects of fractal geometry are present in 12th century castles, Hindu temples, gothic cathedrals, baroque churches and many old towns. Even Neolithic villages appear 'fractal'. How did the builders of old do it? It was a felt thing. They just knew it in their guts. In the same way we find these architectures nourishing and seek them in our leisure times (whilst invariably experiencing much of the present-day standardised, factory-built, fractal-free environment as sterile).

Folk architecture is made up of interrelated similar shapes of different sizes juxtaposed seemingly any-old-how but ordered by the topography of the terrain and everyday needs of their occupants. Such places are analogous to the human brain. The fractal-like folds of our brain's cortex allow its size and complexity to be increased exponentially allowing a lot of grey matter to be packed into a little head. (Imagine the size of head we would need without those folds). So with our traditional dwelling places. Their undulating edges massively increase the total area permitting much more to take place there. The 'permeable' building margins allow an interconnecting network of lanes, footpaths, alleyways, 'cut-throughs', 'snickets', 'ginnels' (there are many local words) criss-crossing, curving, leading this way and that, interpenetrating the spaces between buildings, linking the different areas, making community. Furthermore the 'perforations' are, in those places where we feel at home, of human scale allowing three or four to walk together but not a whole cohort. Hierarchies of scale, the same basic forms in different sizes, repeat again and again as an insistent rhythm. Here we have richness and variety, beckoning views, changes of texture, contrasts of light and shade and a human dimension. There is a certain intricacy in the individual buildings however simple or humble they appear.

We think ourselves progressive but in fact we have lost out. One shining example is the exquisite little medieval pink and cream city of Assisi in the heart of Italy. It is fractal through and through, compact yet 'endless'. Everywhere leads to everywhere else via half-hidden little lanes, curving passageways and 'cat steps'. Things happen in these throughways – artisan workshops and restaurants and homes and people walking and talking. You feel safe, both expanded and enfolded.

Compare that with today's average new estate. Flat, featureless, no place to go. 'Dead ends' speak for themselves. The process intensifies as we block off the old walkways and clog the once open breathing spaces in our towns and cities. Sadly many of us are not immersed in a fractal world in relation to our built environment. New developments are frequently devoid of fractal properties. Cul-de-sacs and no-through-roads allow no 'permeability'. Sameness is not the same as 'self-similarity' and often there is little sense of the integration or 'linkage' which makes for community. Such places, sprawling though they may be, can be claustrophobic and leave us feeling edgy, restless and unsafe. These are important factors for developers to consider. At home, however, by bearing in mind the three fractal properties, we can compensate.

How then may we make our home fractal-rich? We can bring in fractal objects of nature; branches, cones, feathers. We can hang blown up photos of snowflakes or ferns or the night sky on our walls. We can display images of computer-generated fractals. Handmade items are often particularly rich in fractal texture.

To allow a sense of fractal 'permeability' in a too-small room or where we feel hemmed-in, we can create an opening, a stable door or throughway, to an adjoining room. A straight-through niche or hatch may do the same. Open shelves partially replacing walls can offer glimpses into other spaces, throwing their own patterns of light. Even a tiny mirror can 'pierce', visually and symbolically, a too-solid wall.

'Self-similarity' can indicate similar treatment but of assorted scale such as doors and windows of the same style but different sizes. It may mean uniform treatment of details such as picture frames, depth and style of skirting boards or thickness of shelving. It could even mean decorative items grouped by similarity of material, colour, shape, texture, function, theme or metaphor.

Fractal 'linkage' offers a sense of cohesion. We can, for example, go for the same carpet throughout or harmonise paintwork or the treatment of walls.

If we extend our property, we need to keep the fractal dimension in mind. If we add a single storey wing with a pitched roof to our two storey house, the slope of the new roof should be at the same angle as the existing roof. If steeper or shallower, the extension will grate and we may not know why. Similarly if the present roof has a slight flare or overhang this should be reflected in the new roof. The extension then links with the original structure. If we live in a limestone area and our windows are framed traditionally with stone or in a brick area with windows arched in the local manner, any new windows should echo the existing ones. The fractal quality can connect the property to the wider neighbourhood. In one area of Brittany for instance, many doorways are arched. Each such door connects with the others making for cohesion and harmony. If there is a pre-existing fractal quality we should conserve it or enhance it further. This is more about reflecting than exact copying.

We are complex creatures. We need variety and surprise within satisfying wholes in all aspects of our life and present-day building is not, in the main, providing it. The fractal world is untamed and unexpected yet has inherent order. We respond because it feeds the complexity and the unity that we are. Our modern built environment is often bland and smooth and cannot stimulate us neurologically. The implications of this are far-reaching. In honouring the fractal in our surroundings we allow ourselves depth and texture, beauty and harmony, variety and a sense of integration.

The exciting thing is that, with fractals, individually we can make our homes fabulous and collectively we have the potential to create afresh an architecture throbbing with life and vitality.

Composition

The works of a great painter or photographer are composed of and unified by a hidden structure, a sort of invisible skeleton of 'regulating lines' on which the image is hung. Whenever three or more points in an image line up, there is such a line. Harmonious buildings are also living compositions in stone, brick or wood. If you take a photo of any pleasing building, however grand or simple, you can do a magical thing. Draw diagonal lines linking key elements; corners of windows, the lintel over a door, the apex of the roof, a fanlight, a chimney, the point where the corners of walls meet the ground etc. A coherent pattern emerges from the individual lines, for example, a diamond-shaped grid. Often these patterns are complex and multiple though the building may seem plain.

Sometimes the pattern links with some feature outside the building and operates in three dimensions. Do the same with most modern buildings built without heart from factory-made modular units and the patterns are weak or incomplete or consist of a series of lines shooting off every which way; discord with no overall pattern or harmony. *(Bibliography: Hale)*

Take two buildings equally simple. One is 'rich', the other bland and boring. The first has strong regulating lines, the second is devoid of composition or cohesion. Herein lays the difference between genuine Georgian houses and most mock-Georgian reproductions. The old houses have perfect composition, the new frequently none although they purport to be the same.

In the old vernacular architecture these patterns often arose unconsciously. They allow for irregularity and surprise within an overall harmony. Like a beautiful face, their perfection lies in slight variations within a basic form. These are human-scale buildings. They have warmth and texture. We feel welcomed. The contrast is stark between this and the ever-expanding, pretentious, imitative new housing and industrial estates that devour our once green fields. Surely if they could get it right once, we – with all our affluence, know-how and planning officials – could manage it now ... in a contemporary idiom.

Betty Edwards, artist, teacher and author of the classic book 'Drawing on the Right Side of the Brain' demonstrates that the paintings of young children often show an almost flawless sense of composition comparable to that of the most sophisticated world-renowned artists. Mostly, in our hard-edged competitive culture, we lose that sureness of line and form. But we knew it when we were six. It is innate. That is why we respond when we see it in our buildings. We still feel it deep down as we did when we were little, even if we have 'forgotten' it.

When we extend, convert, add new windows or change the façade of a harmonious building, an appreciation of composition is crucial. It is sad, for example, to see a majestic old barn marred when converted into a house because new doors and windows tamper with its inherent composition. Again we don't know what is wrong but we do know it isn't right. Work within the existing pattern and you won't go astray. Adding new pattern is fine providing it is done with the utmost sensitivity.

The built environment exerts a massive, though usually unconscious, effect on us. Building is an immense opportunity and privilege. It is also a great responsibility for what we do now may affect people for decades if not centuries to come.

Ornament

From time immemorial people have decorated their homes inside and out in order to make them beautiful or express some cultural or personal symbolism. Ornament could be fretwork in the timber overhang of a porch, a stone ball on the gable end of an old roof, the arched middle window in a run of three or the carving on a lintel above the front door such as initials or a date stone. I recall a Celtic knot over the door of a new house in West Wales which transforms a 'nice' house into a sensational one.

True ornament is never superfluous. It reinforces the regulating lines of the composition and binds disparate parts of a building into a coherent whole. It can unify the meeting between materials, say brick and glass, or discontinuous structures such as roof and wall. It may connect split elements, as for example with specially crafted handles linking double doors. Often ornament is a simple thickening or raised band or other emphasis of wood or stone. When it draws our attention unconsciously to the underlying geometry it is powerful. It strengthens the architecture and adds to its appeal, though rarely do we know why we feel this attraction. If ornament is at odds with the composition or imposed on a building that has no underlying pattern or added incongruously to an already harmonious façade, it weakens the whole. Importantly, ornament is often functional. A simple wooden post is made beautiful by the brace structure at its junction with the overhead beam. Similarly, and more grandly, a column is most elegant with a capital linking it with the superstructure. Structurally these are important as they help spread the load at stress points. They are not simple add-ons. As ornament they can be modest or ornate as appropriate. And ... they affect our mood profoundly.

Ornament may be carved or painted or embedded in plasterwork but it has nothing to do with mere surface decoration. It is a strengthening and celebration of the inherent qualities of a building, often in highly personal and symbolic ways. The composition must be strong enough to bear such decoration and the ornament should flow with the building and not be extraneous to it. We do well to follow John Ruskin's exhortation in his 'Seven Lamps of Architecture'

(1849) only to decorate construction but not construct decoration.

We need to be cautious but with care and sensitivity ornament can lift a building into another dimension. *(Bibliography: Alexander. Day. Hale. Lawlor)*

Notes

1. When they respond to the laws of Divine Proportion, Fractals, Composition and Ornament, our architecture and internal spaces, however 'simple', feel truly abundant.

2. For new building work, an architect who is sensitive to the power of these four classic imperatives is a must. You are paying. You require nothing less.

Simplicity
& Abundance

More time, more space, a less frantic existence. A full life but a simpler, more meaningful one. Many people yearn for these. The first step may be to clear the clutter, to simplify. As William Morris, pioneer of the Arts & Crafts movement, famously said: "Have nothing in your house that you do not know to be useful or believe to be beautiful". These need be our only guidelines. Do I love it? Do I use it?

Consider each item. If it gives you a buzz or is currently useful, that's great. It has positive energy that supports you. Keep it. As for the rest, offload. Your home is both an ongoing expression of and influence on you. You cannot afford to be surrounded by things that pull you down.

This detox used to be part of the way of life. It was called Spring Cleaning. It took place somewhere around the time of the spring equinox. At 'spring cleaning' every curtain would come down for washing. Each drawer would be scrubbed, sorted and lined with fresh paper. Walls were sponged. The cellar, if you had one, was limed. Everything sparkled inside and out as, at the same time, buds burst on trees and new shoots pushed up through moist earth, the time of primroses and pussy willow. Spring cleaning was, perhaps, a response to some primal urge to renew, refresh and regenerate in tune with Mother Earth.

Today, too often, we have lost touch with the natural rhythms. But clutter-busting, reinvigorating our home in the way that nature does with its green and growing things, still feels good. We are connected at some energetic level with all our possessions. Some enhance our vitality. Others deplete it, even some once-loved items. Our current associations are crucial when de-clogging and revitalising our home.

So what constitutes clutter? What should go so your home, and you, can breathe more easily? Clutter is all that lowers instead of lifts your self-esteem. Clutter is that which does not work and does not fit; the broken, the chipped, the torn, the items never to be repaired. It is the things you are hanging on to because they 'may come in useful' or are around only because they 'cost good money'. It is the clothes that do nothing for you, that you don't wear, the bad buys. It is the paper, old magazines and books that are no longer relevant. It's the 'worst' you are 'using first'. Clutter is everything that provokes ambivalent feelings about people, places, past experiences or your identity. Clutter belongs to and keeps you in some sort of poverty consciousness. It is the stuff that is not current, has no valid currency. It is the junk in your life. It is that which does not represent, reflect and support the essential you as you are in your heart right now, all that is not in tune with where you want to be in your life or where you plan to go.

Would your life be impoverished if a particular item were not there? No? Then it's possibly clutter. What about those never-loved but sentimentally binding items? Sell them. That way the money can go to adorable new things and any sentimental attachment transferred. Remember, you are not honouring a former owner by hanging on to something you dislike or that that owner may have discarded long ago. Unwanted gifts, the presents you never did like but given to you with love, are tricky. The answer is to keep the love but let the item go.

Whilst any time is good to release the old, outworn and outgrown – whether things, habits or unsatisfactory romantic ties – some say the best time is when the moon is waning, that is between full moon and dark of the moon.

The waning moon is a good time to: detox; tend to routine matters; shed emotional baggage; relax and recharge; wind down a project; de-clutter your home. The waxing moon (between new moon and full moon) is a good time to: build your strength; take vitamin and mineral supplements; avoid fattening foods because your body is in an absorbent phase; cut your hair (it will grow more quickly and become even more luxuriant and glossy); put your energy into new projects and creative endeavours; buy a new house.

Clutter affects the flow of energy. Physically it invades space, producing disorder and disharmony. Psychologically it holds unwanted situations in place. The answer to clutter is to let it go so you are surrounded only with things which make you feel good.

The Big Clutter Clear

This is the modern version of the old-fashioned 'spring clean'. It is simple but radical:

1. Take everything out of the room.
2. Refresh the walls, ceiling, floor, woodwork and curtains as necessary.
3. Clean drawers and cupboards.
4. Return only those items you cherish and/or use.

The secret is to be ruthless. Often when you visit the home of newlyweds it is fresh and charming. As the years go by it becomes laden with excess and loses its sparkle. The Big Clutter Clear restores your home to pristine brightness.

The Little Clutter Clear

Whereas the Big Clutter Clear is an occasional activity, the Little Clutter Clear is ongoing. The following clutter clearing sequence makes it easy:

1. **Behind doors**

    Doors are crucial to circulation. When they cannot open fully because of things stuffed behind or hanging on them, there can be an unwholesome feeling of congestion. (Feng shui believes that people who live with partially blocked doors may have trouble seizing opportunities). Clear away anything crowding doors, starting with the front door.

2. **Centres of rooms**

    When the centre of any room is cleared of clutter the space feels larger, airier and fresher.

3. **Corners**

    Corners are where the energy stagnates. Corners are beloved of cobwebs. Corners piled with stuff can be creepy. Clear the clutter.

4. **Horizontal surfaces**

Floors, shelves, tops of cupboards, stairs, window ledges, worktops, tables; all those surfaces where you put things down and there they stay (and mate and reproduce). Clear them.

5. **The unseen**

Drawers, wardrobes, cupboards, lofts, storage areas, under-stair spaces, garages, outhouses. None of us is immune from the disturbing influence of possessions stashed away unseen. Flush the clutter and organise the rest.

6. **Give yourself a treat**

After the clutter clear – a little holiday … some time in nature, visiting a pulsating city, doing a course, whatever … but away for a few days. Come back to a fresh glowing home. Almost always after time away it is easier, even compulsive, to let go even more. Just do it. It's as simple as that. (And the treat is important).

Fashions change. The world changes. We change. Unload what is no longer right for you or wrong for the space. If something has been in the family for five generations but you don't like it, feel free to let it go. Like weeds, which are flowers in the wrong spot, the most exquisite of furniture is clutter in the wrong setting. Allow it to blossom afresh in someone else's perfect place. Have around you only that which you love, supports your present lifestyle, nurtures your self-worth and enhances the space where you are right now. If that leaves you with nothing, start slowly. Release one little something that doesn't do it for you. Then indulge in one thing you adore. A process is started. You will continue to be amazed.

Do not worry about lack. All great artists, poets and designers are ruthless in their work. They pare down and reject everything superfluous. Sublime art is as much about what is left out as what goes in. So with your home. Be brave. Be plain rather than fancy. Be bold rather than itsy-bitsy. You will free up space and time and be rewarded with a lovely supportive environment.

The effect of possessions is immense. The homes of alcoholics, for instance, are often full of childhood reminders. Negative behaviour may arise from patterns rooted in infancy and addiction can be having one's life today held in hock to the past. If your partner is drinking more than is good for them (and you) and their mother's stuff is all over the place, or even one dominant item, maybe that is something that needs addressing. Items of sentimental value are fine but it is essential that each has positive associations and that you love it.

There is one final secret. You want to remain for-ever vibrant? Yes? Then get rid of something. Get rid of something now. Get rid of something often. Allow yourself to move on. De-clutter. Make space. Then there is room for the new and exhilarating to enter into your life.

Simplicity calms and relaxes and helps us feel at peace. Simplicity comes from clear space and organisation. Simplicity's ancient refrain is: 'Less is more'.

Notes

1. **'Creative chaos'**

    Clutter is not the disorder that occurs when work-ing on a project providing it is cleared away when the assignment is completed. Most creative activ-ities generate temporary apparent chaos but there is vitality there quite unlike the dead weight of clutter.

2. **Storage**

    Even the things we love, need and use can quick-ly descend into turmoil when there is no allotted place for them. Good planned storage space is es-sential to help maintain a sense of peace and calm for you to thrive in.

3. **Eyesores**

Eyesores are eyesores because our eyes literally see them and metaphorically get sore. Poor plumbing, wiring, drains and unsightly items which are inescapably there are eyesores. What we should not do is draw the eye to them by trying in vain to beautify or disguise them. The way to deal with eyesores is to merge them harmlessly into their background and/or position eye-catching items to entice the gaze away from them.

4. **The moon – waxing or waning?**

A lunar month is roughly 29½ days. Over this period the moon waxes (seems to grow bigger) and wanes (smaller). For the roughly 14½ days when the moon is waxing, in the Northern hemisphere its convex curve faces right. When it is waning, it faces left.

For the rule of thumb (literally) to tell which part of the cycle we are in, bend your elbows and hold your thumbs horizontally in front of you, thumb tips pointing to each other, nails facing you. See how the thumbnail moons are just like mini half moons in the night sky. In the Northern hemisphere the left thumbnail moon (with its convex curve facing right) mirrors the waxing moon. The right thumbnail moon is like the waning moon. (South of the Equator it's the opposite thumb).

5. Letting go

If there are things you are ready to release – and yet and yet – take photos of them. That way you can recapture the pleasure of them at any time.

(For scientific confirmation of the detrimental effects of a cluttered environment on the brain's ability to focus and process information, see Bibliography: McMains & Kastner)

The Air We Breathe

In recent years two interrelated things have happened in our indoor spaces; firstly the introduction of super-effective insulation and secondly a proliferation of man-made building materials, paints, adhesives, furnishings, fabrics, household products, plastic bags, cosmetic must haves and more. Unfortunately, unseen and unsuspected, many of these emit toxic gases which, because we seal our homes so efficiently, have no means of escape. Overheating and consequent dry air compound the situation.

We, as human beings, also breathe out waste products or 'bio-effluents' into the air; carbon dioxide, acetone, ethanol and so on. Historically, this has been no problem. Buildings constructed of natural materials, with windows that opened wide onto a relatively unpolluted outdoors, ensured the air inside stayed, for the most part, fresh.

These days things are different. Our streets are blighted by greenhouse gases from traffic and industry. The shocking truth, however, is that the air inside is often even more contaminated than the air outside. Scientists have long recognised this but it is less well known by everybody else. 'Sick building syndrome' no longer refers solely to large, new office blocks and corporate buildings. For many of us, it has permeated our kitchens, home offices, living rooms, our very bedrooms. There are dozens of these contaminants or 'volatile organic compounds' (VOCs) emanating from synthetic materials, most with vicious-sounding names such as ammonia, benzene, carbon dioxide, carbon monoxide, formaldehyde, toluene, trichloroethylene, urethane, xylene. Added to this witches' brew, we are bombarded with electro-magnetic radiation (EMR) from computers, mobile phones and electronic equipment and the air is frequently laden with positive ions. (Negative ions have a positive effect on our health and mood. Positive ions have a negative effect). People vary somewhat in their reaction to airborne contaminants. Some are more vulnerable than others. Some are more susceptible to a given pollutant and others to others and reactions differ. But noxious VOCs in the air don't do any of us any good. Dr Bill Wolverton lists some potential symptoms – allergies; asthma; eye, nose and throat irritations; fatigue; headaches; respiratory and sinus congestion and neurological disorders. These cover a huge range of possible reactions, some potentially severe.

Hopefully science and technology (or common sense) will find a way to resolve these problems. In the meantime we can make a gesture by choosing (or insisting on), as and when possible, products that are environmentally friendly. We can also, for instance, help new furniture etc. to offload some of its toxic emissions (to 'off-gas') by leaving it outside for a while. Much of today's merchandise, however, takes years to off-gas and some never does. But help is at hand – and from an unexpected source – NASA. In the early days of space travel, NASA, researching air quality for astronauts, turned to nature. Which are the eco-systems that keep the air consistently fresh all over the planet? One answer lies in green nature – trees and living plants. As we all know, plants absorb the carbon dioxide we exhale and release clean fresh oxygen back into the air.

The NASA research, led by Dr B.C. Wolverton, took this further. Scientists studied the relationship between some common houseplants and air pollutants and found that not only did the plants absorb CO_2 and release oxygen, they mopped up other poisonous gases too, thereby helping – often dramatically – to purify indoor air. Later studies with similar results have been conducted by others such as the University of Georgia and Washington State University.

Many of the plants studied evolved on the forest floor in tropical environments where light is reduced. Their pot plant descendents thrive well therefore in household light and basically like the same conditions as we do. Of the plants tested, the Boston fern is the best remover of formaldehyde, probably the most pervasive of the indoor polluting VOCs. The areca palm is outstanding against xylene and toluene and the lady palm against ammonia, Asparagus ferns are superlative negative ionisers. Some other heavy-duty workers are spider plants for zapping carbon dioxide and peace lilies for bio-effluents. Most plants help in multiple ways. Dragon trees (dracaenae) are brilliant multi-purpose air cleansers. English ivy is probably the best all-rounder for clearing the air of the widest range of harmful chemicals. Grown outside, ivy is one of the best plants for mopping up traffic pollution before it enters your home. (See bibliography for other such plants). Whichever plants you choose (and the wider the variety the better) they are a whole lot more rewarding than electrical negative ionisers and air purifiers.

Many house plants are large and often quite 'architectural'. They can look wonderful, for example, against plain white walls. For feel-good generally, choose soft 'friendly' plants and avoid the sharp, spiky ones and the aggressive-looking ones like Mother-in-Law's Tongue. There is one exception to the 'spiky' rule, the Apple Cactus *(Cereus Peruvianus)*, the recently re-named Computer Cactus. It is a Mexican cactus which is outstanding for soaking up electromagnetic radiation. Nobody knows quite how but it is thought that its spines may act as 'aerials' for EMR, funnelling it down into the plant where it is absorbed. *Cereus Peruvianus* should find a place beside every computer.

Plants can be our allies in other ways too. For instance, should you wish to keep cats away from a certain area, indoors or out, go for peppermint. Cats hate the smell. Conversely, when wanting to attract your kitten to a certain area, enlist catmint which all cats find irresistible. (Outdoors – rabbits, deer, moles, mice and other such visitors are repelled by garlic). In an area infested with house flies, wasps, or mosquitoes, you will find an eau de Cologne plant to be a great friend. If you can't sleep at night, have a chamomile plant and/ or a lavender near your bed. Ignore old wives' tales (and hospital ward rules) about plants in bedrooms. Carbon dioxide exhaled by plants at night is minimal and is far out-weighed by the benefits they bestow.

Of an infinite number of plants, only a handful have been tested for their ability to remove toxic fumes from our indoor spaces but all have impressive air purifying properties. So, choose plants you love, the more of them, the better. Favourite garden plants and herbs in pots, for instance, are lovely indoors and can be planted out later. You can be fairly certain that any plants you choose will help freshen the air and uplift your spirits. An indoor garden has benefits far beyond purification of the air. By bringing plants into the home, we attune ourselves to a powerful, calming, natural, benign force. The plant/human collaboration is ancient and satisfying. There is much to explore.

There is yet another solution. Build an eco-home. *(Bibliography: Day)*. Or retrofit an existing one. (And still enjoy your plants).

Notes

1. For the tender-hearted among you, plants appear not to suffer damage from exposure to VOCs, but actually to thrive. Some even seem to step up their removal of poisonous gases the longer their exposure to them. And for the sceptical, plants have been found not to reach a saturation point where toxins are released back into the air. Our plant allies clean *and continue to clean* the air.

2. 'Biophilia' is a term first used by the psychoanalyst Eric Fromm to mean "the passionate love of life and all that is alive". A few years later in 1984, the biologist Edward O. Wilson proposed the 'biophilia hypothesis', the premise that our attraction for nature and all living things is genetically de-

termined. This is why, he suggests, we feel simultaneously alive and at peace when we are out in nature. A walk in the woods refreshes and recharges us at some strange, deep, spiritual level. This has prompted a whole new field of biophilic design which aims to integrate nature into the structure of our buildings and indoor spaces. An example near me is a large independent farm shop. It has a 'living wall', a whole flat interior wall entirely covered with fresh green plants. This contributes towards an unusually attractive ambience and calm, relaxed shopping experience. *https://keelhamfarmshop.co.uk*

3. Avoid using plastic pots for your plants. Plastic in all its forms is a major offender.

   For detailed information on indoor air pollutants, their sources and effects and for pot plant 'air fresheners' see Bibliography, especially: Wolverton

4. There are now a few small, individual firms producing eco-friendly organic paints in lovely colours. See for example: *www.theguardian.com/lifeandstyle/2009/feb/09/eco-natural-paints-guide-best*

Caution

1. Both for health and to minimise the burning of fossil fuels, go easy on the central heating. Particularly, anything over 72°F/22°C activates indoor chemical fumes and further increases toxic build-up.

2. As a reminder, cigarette smoke is laden with VOCs and 'passive smoking' is seriously bad for us. Vaping is no solution. It also leads to indoor air pollution. See, for instance: *www.ncbi.nlm.nih.gov/pubmed/29288255*

Space Magic

Following are a few more tools of the trade which can be transformational:

Colour – advancing and receding

Colour has many fascinating cultural, psychological, seasonal and religious associations. Colour preferences, however, are individual and instinctive. Some like clear colours, others the half tones we cannot quite name; is it green, is it blue, is it grey? Keeping within your chosen palette you can use colour deliberately to give an illusion of a larger or smaller area or help balance poor proportions.

Advancing colours are those which make a room seem cosier or smaller or which visually shorten a long narrow space if painted on an end wall. These are the warm hues (towards the red end of the spectrum) and dark shades. They give the illusion of bringing the walls in or a high ceiling down. To make a room cosier, use warm, deep, strong, advancing colour.

Receding colours are the opposite. Cool (towards the violet) and pale, they optically expand a space or make a ceiling 'higher'.

White is the definitive 'receder' and black the ultimate 'advancer'. White reflects light and white walls visually enlarge a room more than any other device but may be harsh. Pale blue, the colour of the sky, is the next most powerful room enlarger but can be cold. To make a space feel more spacious, choose white or a pale colour but ensure a warm quality of light and some soft, warm accents in the décor.

The advancing or receding quality can be overridden by its depth so, while pink is warm and advancing and blue cool and receding, an electric cobalt blue is more advancing than a baby-soft pink. This is something to play around with. If you do, you can make dramatic changes in the ambience, apparent size and proportions of any room.

Light

Light is the best mood enhancer of all and is as individual as you are. So let your light shine. Paint with light. Be an artist with light. Be drunk on light. Play with different sources of light; sunlight, north light, electric light, borrowed light, light from the sky, lamplight. See how you can use multidirectional light, pools of light, spot lights, dimmers, coloured light. Consider the different qualities of light. Can you reflect light with mirrors? Will a cut-glass crystal in the window cause rainbows to dance on your walls? Candles and firelight are unsurpassed for creating atmosphere. Flame has a special hold over us.

Daylight is crucial for health. Double glazing absorbs light so we need to optimise the available light as best we can. When light comes from different directions the room picks up its diverse qualities. In the Northern hemisphere we have the calm, constant, north light beloved by artists. The gentle morning sun from the eastern horizon is full of promise for the day ahead. The bright daylong sun from south-facing windows promotes a sense of wellbeing and makes us feel alive. Maybe most beautiful is the evening sun from the west, intimating rest and refreshment, contentment and all good things. The benefit of daylight from multi-aspect windows (windows on more than one wall) is physiological as well as psychological since it allows our circadian rhythms to attune to the changing light. Similarly with artificial lighting, a room illuminated from multiple sources feels altogether more life affirming.

Lighting affects our perception of space. The lighter the room, the larger it feels. By lighting the walls we can make them seem further away and the room feels larger. Up-lighting a ceiling makes it seem higher, again making the room feel larger. Light camouflages corners and sharp edges, making a room feel more spacious. Therefore with light as with colour, we can influence apparent size and shape. Light-reflective surfaces amplify light by bouncing it around, thus making small, dark spaces feel lighter, livelier and larger. If an area feels too vast or 'spacey' (leaving you feeling disoriented and 'spaced out') finishes are best kept matt.

Shadows are the final secret since it is shadow that makes the light sing. Accent lighting is one key to light and shade, allowing washes of light whilst simultaneously, casting interesting shadows. With light and shade you can create any atmosphere at will.

Notes

Wherever possible use or reflect light from the sun. This is important as light deprivation has detrimental effects on our health. (Sunshine is also eco-friendly and free). Roof windows provide light direct from the sky. Sun pipes (solar tubes) too can flood an area with daylight and may be the answer in spaces where neither windows nor roof lights are possible. Importantly they cause minimal night time light pollution. (Blinds can help minimise light pollution from roof lights). Check out 'hybrid solar lighting'. *(For the effects on health of light and light-deprivation, see Bibliography: Hobday)*

Caution

1. Down lighting from individual lamps forming pools of light can be cosy and atmospheric. It is best, however, to avoid ceiling down lighting as sole illumination since it is often harsh and can be deadening. A single central ceiling light draws attention to the middle of the room. The walls are then bereft of interest, the room feels smaller and the whole space is less congenial.

2. Dim light generally needs to be 'warm'. ('Cold' dim light can make a space feel depressing, even distressing).

3. Nowadays we cannot escape large, strident, screamingly harsh, brightly lit institutions, devoid of shadow. It is worth noting that these places exhaust, manipulate and brainwash us.

4. Most important of all is outdoor lighting. In many urban areas light pollution blots out the stars and disturbs the natural rhythms of animal and plant life. Advice on environmentally friendly lighting is readily available. See: *www.britastro.org/dark-skies* and *darksky.org/lighting/lighting-basics*

Lingam stones

Lingams, smooth and oval as eggs, are wonderful for stabilising erratic, 'spacey' energy. They are mysterious stones found in one place only, the sacred Narmada River, high in the Mandhata Mountains, one of the seven holy places of pilgrimage in India. It is thought they fell to earth aeons ago in a meteorite shower. If you saw *Indiana Jones and the Temple of Doom* you will recall that the object of the quest was a sacred stone, a lingam stone. Lingams have a unique mineral composition, a piezoelectric quartz, and are said to have the highest vibration of any stone on earth. This gives them an exceptional ability to focus energy and 'ground' an area. Each lingam is unique, the most prized being those with red markings. The ones generally for sale vary from the size of a small pebble to that of a goose's egg. A 'goose's egg' is the size we need for stabilising a space. Traditionally lingams are anointed with sandalwood oil which maintains their lustre but we can choose any essential oil. Lavender, for example, is lovely. Should you wish to calm a room, place a large lingam there and feel the difference. *(For a fascinating discussion on piezoelectricity, see Bibliography: Church)*

Mirrors

Mirrors are magnificent for the stage management of space yet they are rarely used consciously for this purpose. We tend to stick a mirror on a wall to 'have something there' or because we like its frame or because we do not have the right picture. But mirrors, if used with thought, can change the whole feel of a room.

Large mirrors especially, are useful as they can: make a small space feel bigger; make a dark space feel lighter; reflect light into a room; reflect a view from a window (useful in cramped little rooms); amplify pleasurable views; angle light and views into the room when placed against a splayed window reveal; 'widen' a narrow corridor (especially when placed opposite doors opening into it); 'wake up' windowless, dark or poky rooms, 'dead' areas and tight spaces; 'cool' fiery rooms such as all-red rooms or those with too much technology and too many wires, providing the mirror is not reflecting and 'augmenting' the wires (or indeed anything you find ugly or disquieting); make magic in gardens, especially when half-hidden.

Mirrors are perhaps the most effective way of amplifying light and magnifying space. Generally the larger the mirror, the more transformative its effect. Be brave with mirrors. Be bold. This is not to say that small mirrors do not have a place but for the purpose of making a space feel larger and lighter, go for big.

Notes

1. 'Mirror, mirror, on the wall, who is the fairest of them all?' If you don't like your reflection in a particular mirror, change its angle or its height or the lighting. If it still shatters your self-image, try moving it. If that doesn't do, blame the mirror and kiss it goodbye.

2. Mirrors need to be of the highest possible quality.

Caution

Be vigilant. Mirrors reflecting very strong sunlight can start fires.

Old and new

It is possible to mix and match to great effect. Antique furniture, rugs, paintings etc. can add a sense of stability and calm to minimalist interiors. Cutting-edge contemporary – modern art for instance – may lend excitement to the old.

Round and square

Similarly the combination of round and square can add richness and appeal. For example the contrast of a large square candle placed on a round table is more alluring at a subliminal level than round-on-round or square-on-square.

Round cut-glass crystals
(the universal feng shui quick fix)

Round cut-glass crystals are used extensively in feng shui to harmonise an uncomfortable feel. By modifying, modulating, transmuting, transforming and/or balancing extreme ch'i and discordant architectural features, crystals can calm an agitated atmosphere or enliven a stagnant one. They are therefore equally useful in rooms where we feel stressed and those where we feel lethargic.

Traditionally they are hung on 9in (around 23cm) lengths of red string although most people today prefer clear filament and some like them no more than an inch from the ceiling. They will do their work however you hang them and can be as unobtrusive as you wish.

Cut–glass crystals range from around ½in to 3in (1.25cm to 7.5cm). As with everything in your home you must like them. If you do, don't overdo it. Generally you never want to go above an inch (2.5cm) and usually smaller than that. If too large they disperse too much energy and can feel threatening. The bigger crystals are just for huge rooms. Normally you need only one in a room as ripples from multiple crystals interfere with each other, the exception being in long passages where they can be spaced at intervals of around 10ft (3m).

Here are some situations where you might like to hang a crystal: between doors and/or windows which are directly opposite each other; in long narrow rooms, halls and corridors; in windowless rooms; in windows that are too large or small; in areas which are too large or small; in areas which feel lifeless or too busy; in or over sharp corners; over the bottom step of a steep staircase or one ending opposite the front door (hang well above head height); from beams; where there are drains (as in bathrooms etc.); where the atmosphere feels in need of 'cleansing'; where the space is too tight for other 'cures'.

Notes

1. Wash crystals regularly so they remain diamond bright.

2. Cut-glass crystals and natural earth crystals have opposite attributes which can be harnessed differently. Cut-glass crystals radiate energy. Earth crystals focus energy.

Caution

Crystals in windows where the sunlight is extreme have, I'm told, been known to start fires. This is exceptional but, as with mirrors, take care.

Symbols and symbolism

Symbols affect us deeply, if subconsciously. As the art on our walls nourishes or unsettles us, so too does the symbolism lurking around unsuspected, even in the most mundane objects. It pays to be alert to this. We can, however, use symbolism consciously to our advantage.

There are many creative ways in which to introduce positive symbols. For example, on the walls before decorating you can write 'peace', 'calm', 'welcome' or whatever you wish to embed into your home or perhaps you might paint the yin-yang symbol for harmony or draw an angel for protection. Use the same paint so these motifs will be invisible but still influence the atmosphere subliminally. If building or converting, you could, for instance, insert natural earth crystals into the lintel over your front door. Rose quartz for example symbolises love.

X-factor – the senses

Flowers, candles and bowls of fruit are the easiest, most immediate and probably the most powerful way to make a place feel vibrant, welcoming, fresh, beautiful and cared for. Flowers and fruit change with the seasons and, as they change, need different containers in different places. Thus by such simple means, not only do you add delight and a sense of comfort, you create a whole new ambience. For a quick fix or for pure pleasure, adorn your home with flowers, candles and bowls of cherries.

These are things that *must* be changed (or eaten). Their transience is part of their joy. I had a friend who, when she married, was given a magnificent carved candle. Year after year it stood on her beautiful table, whilst we, her friends, enjoyed wonderful meals with the candle as the centrepiece. It was never lit. Then, suddenly, she died. Tragically young. No one ever enjoyed the flame from her special candle.

Chicago neurologist, Dr Alan J Hirsch recommends fragrant roses for the home. His research indicates that scents can be used functionally for specific effects. The scent of roses, he believes, stimulates happy memories and lifts our spirits. Cinnamon and pine may do the same. The aromas of green apples and cucumber, Hirsch says, make a room feel larger. Lavender has always been used to aid relaxation and research now validates this, demonstrating that its perfume triggers alpha brain waves associated with a relaxed state. In a bedroom, lavender induces sleep. In rooms where you need to be alert such as home offices, lily and violet promote concentration. A violet-scented room is said to enhance learning speed by 17% and a rosemary-scented room to aid memory, potentially by up to 75% for certain categories of memory. The association of rosemary with memory is centuries-old. Shakespeare's Ophelia declares "There's rosemary, that's for remembrance …". Now today, the science shows that in such gentle ways our home can help meet our fluctuating needs. *(Bibliography: Hirsch. Moss et al)*

Sound also affects spatial perception. Sound insulation can make a small, flimsy house feel more solid, safe and maybe surprisingly – spacious. Music affects mood and the space itself takes on its qualities. For older people, exposure to music from their youth results in their becoming physiologically younger in measurable ways. *(See 1979 experiments by psychologist Ellen Langer and the BBC reality show Young Ones' (2010). Bibliography: Langer)*

So go for the X-factor. Flowers, fruit, scent, sound and candles are simple measures which can be taken right now to help you and your home feel marvellous. They may be all you need.

Dream Homes

Threshold

Doors are ever-fascinating because behind each one lies a different world, a world created by those who inhabit it, a world with its own reference points and reality. Crossing the threshold of a new door leads to who knows where?

'Crossing the threshold' is part of our lore, legend and language. The new husband carries his bride over the threshold. Ritual and ceremony have always centred on the crossing of a threshold. In tribal initiation the pre-adolescent male leaves his mother and the secure ground of his childhood. He crosses the threshold into a strange liminal phantasmagoria out of which, if he survives, he emerges a man. Sometimes there are equivalent initiations for girls. Many folk tales have the same theme. The hero leaves his safe mundane existence and crosses a threshold into a fantastical world. There he undergoes bizarre and often alarming adventures. Re-crossing the threshold, he returns bearing gifts. For us, the theatre can be such an experience. We cross the threshold, whether into a tiny local theatre painted black and purple or into some grand gilded metropolitan edifice. Once there, we suspend our normal way of being and enter a dimension where anything is possible. And hopefully we emerge bearing gifts.

The threshold then is of great significance, not only architecturally but also symbolically. It has entered our psyche. A threshold, technically, is the doorway itself plus the areas outside and inside it. The main threshold of your home is the portal between the public world outside and your private realm within.

Feng shui and vernacular architecture have always understood the significance of the threshold, particularly that of the main entrance. Through it the life energy flows into your home. You, your family, friends, food, mail, news, opportunities, parcels and helpful people, all pass through. You offer your gifts back to the world by re-crossing the threshold. We will look at the door and the area inside it later. For now, let us consider the threshold area outside the front door.

The front entrance should be unmistakably the front entrance. People must know where to go. Best is when there is some transitional space, however small, between the road and the house to allow a little time to adjust. The transition is heightened if subtle features make it as discontinuous with the street as possible. There can be a change of the surface upon which you tread, a change of level, a change of direction, a change therefore of view and light quality, a difference of sound. Such subliminal cues help soften the transition from outside to inside and make it special.

Imagine the street. The light is a certain way, perhaps a bit harsh on this hot dusty day. You enter a different space. The light changes. It is calmer, quieter, filtered through foliage. You knock on the door. The door opens and for a moment your eyes adjust to the relative darkness. You pass into a light-filled house, different again from the light in the street and the light in the garden. This transition is such a sensual experience. We should make it work for us more often.

Where possible, a separate footpath to the front door, distinct from the main drive, leads on effortlessly, avoids confusion and heightens anticipation. It is often the more inviting if it curves. It needs to be wide enough for two and bordered only by 'friendly' plants (no thorns to get tangled up in).

Lighting promotes safety and creates enchantment. Seating around the door suggests hospitality. Even where there is insufficient space for a footpath; symbols of welcome such as fragrant plants, lamps, lanterns, wind chimes or water can enhance and draw attention to the entrance to your home. An evergreen myrtle by the door with its scented foliage is a symbol of love, peace and immortality and is said to bring good luck and a happy home life. A bay tree either side of the door or a pair of benign sculptures are traditional 'greeters'. Space permitting, some shelter from the wind and wet is comforting for guests whilst they are waiting for you to come to the door and for you when you are searching for your key.

If you use other thresholds to enter and leave your home, make them wonderful too. Each becomes your welcome when you return home and sets the tone for your day when you leave. Always greet yourself with beauty and light, not with darkness and clutter.

It is a truism among estate agents that kitchens and bathrooms are the clinchers. There is, however, something even more crucial; something subtle. It is first impressions. And last impressions. These set the mood for the whole place. It's what everyone takes away with them. The cliché goes that most people when buying a house have 'bought' it (or not) before they even step inside. At a deep level 'kerb appeal' is the quality of ch'i around the house, the vital energy which people sense when they say: "I like this house". Importantly it helps determine what *you* feel about your home. The best description I know is that of Terah Kathryn Collins who says that the front entrance should 'en-trance'. It should be entrancing. *(Bibliography: Collins)*

The threshold experience is, ideally, one of the great delights of homecoming and for all who visit.

Door

It was a little rough stone house up a mountain on the remote and rugged west coast. The view was numinous, otherworldly, 'charged'. The only problem was that the view into the house through the glass front door was equally impressive. There was no hall, no lobby, no transitional space, nothing separating outside and inside. The door opened straight into the one and only living room. The postman, the woman collecting for charity, unexpected guests, unwanted visitors, all could see into the room and whoever was there and whatever they were doing before they themselves were spotted. There was no wandering around in the nude in that house. If the house wasn't tidy, and invariably it wasn't, all and sundry knew it. No relaxing of any kind in that house.

The front door of your home is there first and foremost to offer protection and privacy. Your home is your sanctuary and the right front door keeps it that way. It needs to be strong and solid. A good wooden door is both. It is up to the job. A glass door leaves you vulnerable and gives no subliminal feeling of safety. Always you need to be in command of your space. The perfect front door is sturdy, classical and made of timber. Welcoming. Handsome. Gracious. If a glazed door is the only source of natural light, consider changing to timber and installing a sun pipe.

The front entrance, classically, is regarded as the key feature of any building. It is prominent. It proclaims itself. It is there to make a statement. In practice front doors are not always easily visible and then, as a visitor, you feel some confusion as you look for the door, maybe a little embarrassment and perhaps some irritation. Sometimes you go away and forget the whole idea. The archetypal front door, on the other hand, is gloriously, beautifully, inviting … good to come home to and special for those who visit.

There are numerous ways to highlight the door and a makeover appropriate to the house and neighbourhood can change a dull door into an enticing entrance. A well-lit door pulls people towards it. A door in the shade needs some help. Features which block the view of the door, or easy entrance through it, are problematical. Overgrowth needs to be pruned and structural elements may be best dismantled. External framing, as often seen in older houses, adds definition and makes a door appear more substantial. Sometimes it is possible to enlarge the door surround, structurally or decoratively, to great effect. Good door furniture adds emphasis. If brass, let it be shining bright. A door is often accentuated more effectively with bells and numbers to the side as this helps 'widen' the door and maintain its simplicity. Timber doors slashed to take a letterbox often look strangely disfigured. They are psychologically less solid, less impervious. Instead, mailboxes may be better on or through a wall.

Doors are intriguing when set back a little. They invite you. You want to know what is beyond. This, however, presents a paradox. The inset door is not always easily seen and may need special care to help emphasise it. My own favourite front door is quite low but very wide, a lovely simple thick painted old door slightly inset in its solid stone surround. It has a wondrous bell with an iron pull-handle linked to a conventional bell inside which resounds throughout the house. The bell, fresh paint and gleaming door furniture ensure that this door captures your attention despite being recessed.

Measures such as these, together with plants and the other threshold greeters, can transform the dreary into the dreamy. Use your front door at least some of the time. Encourage your guests to use it. It is the main access for people and blessings into your home and sets the scene for all that lies ahead. The whole house is energised when it is used regularly.

Sometimes we replace old front doors with new doors. A few are beautiful. Many more are fancy and pretentious. Some are timber to be true but so processed as to seem inorganic with nothing of the tree left in them. Such doors extend no welcome. Some have a fake half-moon fanlight. Traditional fanlights are set *above* the door; elegant, interesting, individual – lovely examples of architectural ornament.

Even more uninviting are the white uPVC doors and their brown plastic mock-wood sisters. There is nothing more of a killer to a house and its locality than these white plastic and shiny-chocolate imitation timber doors. Their framework is disproportionately bulky and the doors therefore so narrow that some manufacturers have had to redesign their sofas, doing away with comforting high backs because they won't go through.

Often in older houses the most appropriate door is the one already there. If it is ugly or beyond help, the best solution may be a good reclaimed old door or craftsman-built new door, as appropriate.

Walls directly ahead of a door should be a reasonable distance away. This is particularly important with the front door. The rule of thumb is that a wall facing the front door is at least 6ft (about 2m) away. 'In your face' walls give the sense of blocking you. A receding colour is a must on all too-close walls. A 'painting with depth' may help. A large mirror can offer an illusion of distance. Caution here: the wall must be far enough away. You don't want to be bumping into the mirror, saying hello to yourself and wondering how come you banged your head.

Split views, meaning a close-up wall on one side and an extended view on the other, are always unsettling but especially so at this point of entry. Whilst distance may be given to the wall as above, the 'absent wall' will benefit from some suggested barrier such as light curtaining, furniture or plants. These are ways of dealing with split views in any situation.

All doors are about passage. To allow fluid unfettered movement they must be wide enough (in scale with the building or room) and free to open the full 180° without being blocked by a wall or a stash of clutter behind them or clothes hanging on them.

A home often seems more homely when doors are of differing heights and widths, when the door is made to fit the space not the space to fit the door. Hierarchy of scale is important. Ideally the front door is larger (or enhanced to be more eye-catching) than other doors. A generously built front door is more inviting than a little mean narrow one. Inside, if we want to emphasise one room over another we can give it a bigger door to attract people towards it. Size is a subliminal indicator of what is where. It is better that people don't go wandering into your broom cupboard instead of your living room. Size matters with doors.

Nothing in this book is a rule though, merely a guideline. Some of the most fascinating doors of all are tiny, where you have to pause a moment and bend to enter. But these are special cases. The ideal door allows unobstructed passage. It is inviting, welcoming and made of wood. It is solid and protective and gives you privacy. Your front door imparts character and individuality to your home. It sets the mood. It is loved and cared for. And it is used.

Notes

1. Make sure all new wood comes from ecologically managed woodland.

2. Reject virgin rainforest timber.

3. uPVC stands for unplasticised polyvinyl chloride. Internet information abounds, for example this from Greenpeace: 'The production and disposal of PVC-u ... leads to the release of highly poisonous chemicals which threaten the environment and human health. PVC-u production involves no less than six of the fifteen most hazardous chemicals listed by European governments for priority elimination'. *www.greenpeace.org.uk*

Hall

The space into which you first step whether lobby, hall, back entrance or room is the place of greeting. It is the place of arrival. You walk up to the door, you cross the threshold and now you are here. 'Here' needs to be a good place. This is the entrance to your home, your safe haven, the place you can be you.

Space permitting, there is a hall or entrance lobby so you don't step straight into a living area. Ideally there is a lobby and a hall, a continuation of the threshold experience. The significance of such a 'decompression zone' is seen in shops. Any effort to use the entry area for sales is ineffective, even counterproductive. Banks, who more than anyone understand cost-benefit, don't attempt to take your money or even push their pamphlets on you before you have had time and space to psyche yourself up. Invariably we need a moment to adjust when stepping from one space meaning one thing to another space meaning another.

We don't, however, live always and forever with every ideal in place so, if we do find ourselves entering straight into a main room, it is good to recognise the need for a small interlude, maybe with a chair by the door or some other token of quiet welcome. Many houses front straight onto a road and there is little scope for outdoor transitional space. Apartments can have the same problem. It is extra important when nothing can be done outside to provide the 'welcoming pause' within.

Halls are the welcoming spaces not only for our guests but also for us. Emphasis should be on creating a sense of warmth. Terah Kathryn Collins says: "Traditionally, the best painting in the house was hung in the foyer or near the front door as the 'greeter' to honor guests and make a pleasing first impression". Art that gives an appropriate and inviting message can create atmosphere and anticipation for what lies beyond.

Art may also be used to give a subliminal sense of direction so visitors go where you want them to go. It is interesting that, almost always, we look right first and turn in that direction but you may want guests to turn left or go straight ahead. The thing that makes them do that can be as subtle as a painting of people looking, birds flying or fish swimming in your preferred direction (directional art). Or, a well-placed light or other attractive item can seize the attention so people automatically turn and move towards it. Rugs angled a certain way lead you on. You rarely register the rug but automatically follow its path.

What you notice first, determines the feel of the whole house. A living room seen first sets the mood on relaxation and that is usually the ideal. A home office may scream work. If on a diet and you see straight into the kitchen you might find yourself a bit weak-willed in that department, or if there are several rooms competing for attention you can feel disoriented. To make the layout work, attract the eye to certain rooms and away from others.

We need only bear in mind the importance and special nature of our entrance space, the moment of adjustment, the comfort, the daily rite of passage as we step into (and out of) the inner sanctum of our home.

Window

If eyes are windows of the soul, windows are eyes of the home, eyes of the soul of the home. In fact windows are the eyes of the soul of a whole community. I worked once in a place which called itself a village. Although in the heart of Britain's newbuild urban sprawl, the village houses and few shops were graceful 'turn of the last century' buildings, each a little different from the next but part of an overall harmony. The place had character, a nice feel to it. By the time I left, the feel-good was largely gone, gone because of the windows. Spacious Edwardian houses and small Victorian cottages had fallen prey to the double glazing salesman. Nothing else had changed, just the windows and doors, but what had felt good no longer felt so good. Old is not necessarily best but with windows in older houses it often is. Not only did the new estates have identical fake-wood windows upstairs and down and round the corner, now the old village houses were similarly afflicted. One by one the old windows disappeared and new synthetic 'improvements' straight from the uPVC production line took their place. They were uniformly clumsy white plastic or shiny brown contraptions adjusted to fit the non-standard window openings but otherwise carbon copies of each other with little top window panes allowing minimal opening and large panes below, most unable to open at all. Draught-proof. Sound-proof. Burglar-proof. Paranoid windows feeding the paranoid nature of our contemporary culture. It is perfectly possible to provide double glazing and security without destroying the ambience of the whole vicinity. Specialist firms and good local carpenters using timber from sustainable woodland can provide exact copies of original windows with fine, delicate frames and glazing bars. The cost is more, although often not that much more, but worth it. It is better to make do for now and save up for good timber frames which will grace your home and enhance the neighbourhood. uPVC is to be avoided at all costs. Not only is it lifeless, it is environmentally harmful.

External definition of windows, as with doors, accentuates their importance and beauty. Indoors we frame windows with curtains, but simple timber framing also adds character, not only to a window but to the whole room.

A window's most obvious function is to allow in daylight and the light from multi-aspect windows is the most congenial of all. Tall windows are often better for light quality because they reflect more sky. Upstairs rooms tend to be lighter, sometimes making 'upside down living' (living rooms upstairs/bedrooms downstairs) an attractive option. Light quality is one reason why penthouse flats are so costly.

Ventilation, historically, was the first function of windows and open windows are still the prime source of healthy ventilation. Cross-ventilation is particularly important in hot weather and, with global warming, will be ever-more crucial. Multi-aspect windows which open fully are the best and most satisfying way of achieving this. It is becoming just as important to cool our homes in summer as to heat them in winter … and with minimum environmental impact. Open windows on more than one side of the room allowing a free flow of air are infinitely more pleasant than air conditioning.

View, a window on the world, is the other function of windows. From our safe 'refuge' within, windows give 'prospect' onto the world without. A tantalising view from a small window is often more enticing than an ever-present dominant one from a huge picture window so, for comfortable ambience, several smaller windows may be preferable to one mammoth one.

This allows a greater number of views with increased interest and more diffuse light. Softening of overly large windows may be achieved by subdividing them into multiple panes. The outlook from every window needs to be as beautiful as possible, though beautiful is not always possible. Sympathetic window treatments – flowers, candles, window boxes – may do much, however, to mellow an unforgiving view.

Whilst you want to see out onto the world this should not be at the cost of privacy. Sometimes it is necessary to find ways of screening yourself from prying eyes, for example with plants on windowsills, 'café curtains' or, if needs must, one-way mirror glass. Simply re-routing a garden path may ensure privacy. You need to see people coming to your house without them first seeing you.

Associated with light is colour and a lovely way of introducing colour into a room is with plants, leaves and flowers at the window. They filter and soften the sunlight as it enters the room. The leaves glow green and translucent and the walls inside come alive. Candle flame reflected in windows also speaks of warmth, welcome and hospitality. In some rural areas of Ireland a lighted candle in a window is, traditionally, a gesture of welcome, food and a bed for the night.

Otherwise windowsills are often best left clear as ornaments tend to block light and view and detract from the serenity of the room. Anything that *is* placed on a windowsill should look as good from outside looking-in as from inside looking-out.

We gravitate to light as we do to warmth and window seats beckon us to sit, pause awhile and dream. They are redolent of an earlier, more unhurried way of life, allowing us to be in touch simultaneously with the world beyond and with whatever is happening inside. There are other ways too of transforming a window into a place which will invite us to draw up a chair, to read, to eat, to chat. How pleasurable is a kitchen for instance, when we can sit by the window instead of washing up there. Low windowsills, a ledge where we can place a drink, maybe a little table ... all help make a window more than a functional light giver. 'Low' can be 12in-14in (around 30–35cm) above the floor at ground level but 20in minimum (about 50cm) upstairs for safety and a 'feeling' of safety.

Perhaps the worst aspect of much modern plastering is seen in windows. Many houses today have right angled window reveals with knife-edged corners. The incoming ch'i is then deflected, laser-like, as poison arrows. Plastering needs to be soft around windows. The splaying of window reveals eliminates the sharpest angles. Not only does this make the windows more attractive but it spreads more light (with less glare) and rooms feel more spacious and congenial. Splaying is as relevant in new houses with thin walls as in old, thick-walled houses where it is traditional. When splaying is not possible, timber window surrounds and reveals can soften the ambience and add interest.

Because they determine the quality of light, windows enliven an interior more than any other structural feature. They express the spirit of the home and influence the feel of the whole locality. As with doors, they should be in keeping with the style of the house and character of the neighbourhood. Given the importance of windows, structural improvements are often the best option. This can entail adding windows, repositioning, changing size or style, making them higher to gain more light, lowering windowsills for added charm, splaying window reveals, replacing thick new clumsy glazing bars with more delicate ones and so on. Be sensitive, however, to the external composition of the building and remain in sympathy with any period detail. Replacement of original sash windows needs to be to the original specifications. Any other window looks wrong, jars on the vicinity and devalues your property.

The right windows will improve your home, enhance the neighbourhood and add value to your property.

Note

Multi-aspect windows are a key feel-good feature – perhaps *the* feel-good feature – softening glare and imparting a certain magic as the light slides round, caressing one wall then another. They allow lovely through-ventilation and offer multiple views. If you are designing or re-designing a house, dual or multi-aspect windows are one of the first things to think of.

Ceiling

Have you ever lived in a house with exceptionally low ceilings and tried to sell it? A couple come to see it. They say they adore it. Then almost on the point, you think, of sealing the deal he bumps his head on a beam. The sale is lost. Inevitably.

There is a range of ceiling heights with which we are generally most comfortable. Too low and a space is claustrophobic. An overly high ceiling can disorientate. We need to feel contained but not oppressed.

With the exception of very large rooms in palatial houses, the ideal ceiling height is considered to be around 8ft–10ft (around 2.5m–3m). This is not to say that ceiling heights should necessarily be the same throughout. A house with variable room heights is always intriguing.

It is noteworthy (and useful in the zoning of space) that in two rooms of identical length and width but differing heights we perceive the space differently. The higher room feels larger and more formal and we seem further apart. The lower room seems smaller and more intimate and we feel closer together. 'Active' rooms such as home offices can take some extra height. 'Quiet' areas may be somewhat lower. Thus through ceiling height, the structure can be differentiated in a way that is conducive to differing life pursuits and fluctuating daily rhythms. This is especially helpful in open plan layouts where, together with differing floor levels, a variety of ceiling heights within the 'comfortable' range can help define living areas, giving each a special feel and adding interest to otherwise uniform and boring spaces. There is, of course, always room for the exception. In an otherwise balanced house, extremes of ceiling height may add exciting drama or agreeable intimacy. You can drop quite low to create a cosy retreat or differentiate an alcove. A cathedral ceiling can be stunning. There are few hard and fast rules in life.

It is astonishing how much difference an inch or two higher, a few centimetres lower, makes to the apparent size of a room. Newbuild houses and old cottages are often uncomfortably low. To 'raise' a ceiling, let it be white, semi-reflective and well lit. To 'lower', use warm, strong, matt colour, even down to picture rail level.

We need light in our homes. Light makes us feel good. Light makes any space more inviting. Light lightens our mood and lifts the atmosphere. The ceiling is crucial, reflecting and amplifying light – or deadening it. Textured ceilings are the big killer. They absorb a massive amount of light, making the room darker and more oppressive. Fortunately it is simple to skim over a ceiling.

Beams are much favoured, much in vogue. 'Exposed beams' are a selling point. But beams are regarded differently in feng shui. They are seen as adding not character but a sense of the colossal weight of the building which they are supporting. Subliminally we are aware of this. The bigger, heavier, darker, closer together or lower the beams, the more ominous our interpretation of them at this unconscious level. In fact it is claimed that prolonged periods with one's head under a beam can cause headaches. Beds, dining tables and sofas should be moved away from the influence of a beam. What we really love about old beams is the beauty of the hand-cut timbers, the softened edges, their individuality. There are many ways, however, of introducing the hand-wrought, the original and the one-off.

Beams are seen also as channelling strong lines of ch'i which act negatively against us, as confirmed by muscle tests. Everyone tests weak compared with their normal strength when standing under and at right angles to a beam. (The same happens for example when directly opposite sharp corners or in the presence of clutter and unloved belongings) This is significant. Our environment really does affect our intrinsic energy. *See note below on muscle testing.*

To minimise the adverse effects of beams we can 'lighten' them both in colour and apparent weight by, for example, lime-washing them in the traditional manner. Garlands of greenery help soften them. Sharp edges can be chamfered, though any sanding of beams (or any old wood) needs to be by hand as mechanical sanders are too vicious and destroy the natural beauty of the wood. Given adequate height, lightweight objects ('sky art' such as mobiles, feathers, gauzy textiles) hanging from beams help counteract the heaviness. A traditional feng shui method is to place two bamboo flutes diagonally at 45° angles on the side of a beam so the 'sound' from each flute 'floats up' to mingle with that of the other. The desired effect is to lift and circulate the ch'i. Alternatively you could find some way of your own, for example by substituting angels for the bamboo flutes. Structurally, if the ceiling is high enough, the beams can be enclosed. Or some beams only can be covered, creating variation in ceiling height to differentiate separate areas.

Other undesirables add subliminal threat from above. Ceiling fans should be avoided wherever possible. From an energy perspective they chop the ch'i too violently. If over a dining table they can make people irritable, argumentative and inclined to gulp down their food at speed. Chandeliers and fans above breakable objects, furniture and particularly over beds are hazardous. Kitchen utensils hanging from trendy overhead racks are interpreted by the psyche as potential or impending peril. Knives are better on wall racks or better still, stored out of sight. These are actual as well as perceived dangers. If they come adrift from their moorings, you are in hospital.

Our homes are primarily refuges, places where we can recharge and be ourselves. Ceilings can offer just the right amount of containment or they can impart a sense of limitation or leave us too wide open. They can calm or threaten us. And mostly we are oblivious as to why we feel as we do. There is, perhaps, no feature that gives this message of security without oppression, or the lack thereof, more than the ceiling.

Notes

1. Ceiling height

High ceilings promote inspiration, creativity, abstract thinking, contemplation and meditation. Lower ceilings are better for concrete thought and focussed detailed work. *(Bibliography: Anthes.*

Lidwell) Why else would artists choose lofty garrets, monks build soaring abbeys and accountants do your books in a workaday office? This also questions the potentially stultifying effect of the very low ceilings in so much newbuild UK housing. There is a Bedouin saying, "When you sleep in a house your thoughts are as high as the ceiling, when you sleep outside they are as high as the stars."

2. Beams and Rafters

'Beams' as referred to above indicate the straight projecting timbers which cut across the ceilings of (usually low) rooms. These are very different from the hand-crafted upward-rising, often naturally curving rafters of many old structures such as larger houses, churches and barns. Fortunately there are still a few (a very few) master craftsman building contemporary homes in the old way with, for example, green oak frames and timber pegs instead of nails. Such new buildings are uplifting, inspiring and environmentally friendly.

3. Muscle testing

Claims made in these pages, such as those relating to beams, can be verified by muscle testing. Here is an easy method which shows instantaneously how differing conditions affect our deep energy. Ensure the person you are testing is nice and relaxed. Ask them to stand with their arm stretched to the side, hand at shoulder level, palm facing down. Place your hands lightly on their outstretched arm, one hand between the wrist and elbow and the other on the same-side shoulder to stabilise it. Invite them to make their arm 'strong'. Once 'locked in', apply reasonable downward pressure on their forearm for a couple of seconds. Usually they resist your force easily. Let them think of something pleasant (they need not say what they are thinking). Then press down smoothly. Their arm may be even stronger. Ask them to think of something currently troubling them and the arm will lose its power to resist and crumple under your pressure.

For testing the effects of the built environment, say sharp corners, first test your friend in a pleasant open place. Ask them to 'think their arm strong' and they will probably test strong. Then test them facing a 'poison arrow'. Their arm will almost certainly collapse, unable to withstand your light pressure. When muscle testing, keep the pressure smooth and continuous. Ask if your pressure is comfortable or whether it needs to be a little softer or stronger and adjust accordingly. If a subject tests weak for pleasant *and* unpleasant they may be dehydrated and badly in need of a glass of water.

Importantly, always end each muscle testing session on a 'strong' result.

Muscle testing taps into the life force and can access our inner wisdom about anything. Since our environment affects our deep energy (as confirmed by muscle tests) we owe it to ourselves to make our surroundings the most congenial we can. If uncertain about a part of your home or its effect on you, muscle test it.

Staircase

anic. Suddenly it happens. On the Leaning Tower of Pisa. Paralysed. Transfixed in terror. Stuck. Can't go up. Can't go down. But can't spend the rest of my life halfway up the Leaning Tower of Pisa. But to avert that possibility is an impossibility. It means letting go my hands which are clinging desperately onto something, turning round, then descending. Help, as ever, is at hand. But the anguish is real.

I am not alone. A gut-wrenching fear of heights and steepness of gradient is common. If you suffer, you may have felt a hint of this at the top of a long steep staircase. You look down. Vertigo threatens. Of course it is manageable. You control it. But you don't like it. Flashbacks to films where the heroine crashes to her doom flit briefly across your mind. You clutch the rail, glad you have not had too much to drink tonight.

Feng shui sees everything in terms of its ch'i or energy quality and uses the analogy of water. Ch'i prefers to meander like some slow, sinuous, sleepy stream. Staircases are challenging. The ch'i cascades down. A steep straight narrow staircase feels like Niagara and you don't want to be riding the rapids there. The landing is 'pulled on' and offers no sense of protection. Nor is it peaceful downstairs. It is as though the energy is forced down the stairwell, flooding furiously into the space below. Worst is when the steps end immediately opposite the front door, a sure sign according to feng shui that your finances are flotsam, hurtling down and right out the door. Ditto your health. Even in everyday terms, steep staircases and/or those opposite the front door are not feel-good features. Fear not. There are things you can do.

One way to mitigate a dangerous sense of gradient is to accentuate the horizontal. Strong horizontal lines can be created with, say, painted borders or suggested by pictures with their tops at the same level (not sloping down along the length of the staircase). Handrails painted to blend with the walls help minimise the sense of downward pull. Art evoking lightness, buoyancy and upward mobility counterbalances it. At the bottom, a restful painting on the wall or large mirror reflecting back the staircase or a nice thick rug can add a sense of security. Space permitting, a visual protective barrier (plants, a screen etc.) can help ameliorate the poor design of a 'directly opposite' staircase and front door.

A tight, narrow, closed-in staircase feels oppressive. White/very pale walls, large mirrors and stair carpets with horizontal stripes help give an illusion of greater width. It is often more congenial, however, for an enclosing wall to be replaced with banisters, one bonus being that the downstairs space feels more spacious. Sometimes the best long-term staircase solution is a re-design to allow a turn and shallower, more forgiving steps.

Feng shui regards spiral staircases as unfortunate with their blade-like steps cutting the energy and dispersing it helter-skelter every which way. They act like downward-sucking whirlpools. When in the centre of a room, they are seen in feng shui as correlating with heart problems. Nor are spiral staircases necessarily space-savers as building regulations often stipulate quite a wide base for them. And how are you going to get furniture up and down? And people with bad legs? Importantly, spiral staircases negatively affect resale.

With a spiral staircase, the priority is to counter-act the vertiginous, vortex-like sensation. The central pole can be a different colour from the steps. Upward-growing plants in heavy terracotta pots around the base of the staircase help, the plants since they suggest upward movement and the terracotta because it is 'earthy' and 'grounded'. The best answer by far, however, is to replace with a conventional staircase.

Keep the stairs clear of clutter that blocks easy movement. Ensure good lighting, non-slip treads and good handrails. Safety is crucial but so is a feeling of safety. Never opt for open risers. They do not feel safe.

A generous landing creates enormous individuality and character whilst offering a period of adjustment from downstairs to up. A window not only adds interest to the landing but illuminates the staircase and throws light from another direction into the space below. A window seat or chair by the window is even better. Downstairs, height as well as light can be 'borrowed' from above.

Many houses have too little storage room but the under-stair area is often a vast untapped reservoir of useful space. Sometimes this can be maximised if given more than one access point and/or if the lowest steps are constructed as drawers or hinged to open upwards, either way providing storage below the treads.

If you have a less than lovely staircase you can transform the whole feel simply by changing the banisters. Replacing mass-produced curvy spindles with, for example, simple straight ones can be transformational.

Staircases at their best are key connecting areas. Ideally they have easy bends and shallow steps and are wide enough. They are open to and an integral part of the room or entrance space. They provide friendly places to sit and chat at a party especially if they fan out a little at the bottom. They offer a comforting sense of cohesion to a building. They hint at different levels of being and allow a sense of integration. Make the most of them.

Bedroom

The bedroom deserves a section to itself since it is quite the most important room. Home is where we go for R&R. And most of all it is in the bedroom where we rest, relax, recuperate and recharge – and maybe read. All the R's. And the S's too. Sleep, serenity, sensuality. That's what bedrooms are for. Often when people buy a new home they decorate little by little, leaving the bedrooms until last because they are not on view. Your bedroom should be the first place to start making your home your own.

Quintessentially, the main bedroom needs to be intimate and private, calm but sensuous and the guardian of equality. Ideally it is located at the back (or quietest part) of the house.

Intimacy calls for the room to be the right size, neither too small nor too large. There is a saying in feng shui: 'The bigger the bedroom the higher the divorce rate'. This is because it is harder to make a large room feel secluded and comfy. It is possible but requires care. A too-large bedroom can be rendered cosy and snug with warm colour, soft fabrics and gentle lighting. Perhaps separate areas for sitting and sleeping can be suggested or a walk-in closet carved from the space. If on the other hand a bedroom is tiny, a low bed, pale walls and absence of extraneous items will help make it seem more spacious.

Privacy, actual and subliminal, is essential. Keep photos of children, parents (and the rest) out of the bedroom. All those eyes on you. It's a no-no. Nor is this the place for images of spiritual guides and religious themes. There are plenty of places for your precious people and icons. Your bedroom isn't one of them.

Indulge your senses. Enhance the room with music, art, candlelight, essential oils, beautiful bed linen, textiles, rugs and a few (not too many) soft cushions. In your bedroom it is especially important that each item has only good associations, thoughts, feelings and memories. Art can be serene or sensual, tender or erotic, the only criterion being that you adore it. Items over your bed head must be lightweight and securely attached to the wall with nothing loose or sharp. Not only must they be safe, they must feel safe. Lighting should be soft, warm and romantic. You must, of course, be able to make the room deliciously dark at will, day or night, so choose window coverings that are up to the job. Mirrors activate space and removing them (or covering them at night) calms a bedroom instantly.

And more than anywhere, colour is critical in the bedroom. Often in TV house makeovers and magazine articles a bedroom will be pale blue. We all know blue is calming. But blue is not warm and indulgent. In the bedroom it is the wrong colour in the wrong place. Colour literally colours the mood of a room. In a friend's home the guest room is furnished with beautifully sinuous, rich-toned French antiques with a wonderful patina. Previously the walls were white and a large disquieting painting hung opposite the bed. Sleep seemed ever-evasive. Then one day the picture was gone and the walls were the colour of molten amber. Instead of stark white, now there is a golden, orangey, syrupy, glowing, deeply cocooning warmth. I cannot tell how blissful the experience of sleeping there.

So which colours to choose? Basically you need warm, comforting, libido-friendly shades. Forget the cool tones except as small touches. You can go baby pale, mysterious dark or voluptuous rich, thus allowing an enormous range from hint-of-a-tint to full-on; the pinks, the butter creams, the golden rosy apricots, the lemons and golds, the rusts and russets, the aubergines, the clarets and, above all, skin tones. Skin-on-skin offers the greatest comfort of all as we know from infancy. If we consider all the possible variations of skin tones we come up with a vast array of sumptuous hues.

To avoid are the cool colours: chaste white and the greys and blues and greens and grey greens and grey blues and of course, black. If stuck with them for the time being, make sure the lighting is warm and bring in warm accents in the form of bedcovers, cushions, throws, rugs, paintings. There is such a wealth of se-ductive sunlit colour to enfold you in deep caressing warmth. Enjoy.

The main bedroom needs to demonstrate equality in all ways. For example on both sides of the bed there should be space, a bedside table and individually ad-justable lighting.

In the name of tranquillity ban all 'equipment' from the bedroom. Avoid desks or anything that suggests ac-tivity, work or things to be done. The telephone too can intrude and it may be better in non-urgent situations to disable it at night. If you must watch television in bed, put the set to rest when not in use. Store it in a cupboard or cover with an attractive textile or lean a favourite painting against it. Televisions are, however, better out of the bed-room. 'Blue-white' LED lights, computers, digital clocks, smartphones, tablets and screens of all types are unwise in bedrooms. Many people find their sleep disturbed and don't know why but the fault lies with an electronic light-emitting device. It is thought that blue-white light at night interferes with the natural production of mela-tonin needed for sound sleep. Instead, bedroom lighting needs to be warm and cosy. Additionally, for those times when you wake in the middle of the night and switch on a light but want to get back to sleep gently and easily, dim red light (say from a bedside lamp) can be soothing. The red light will not jar your system nor have the same negative melatonin impact.

Feng shui is not fond of en suites which open di-rectly into the bedroom because of their energy-sap-ping drains and plug holes. Having an extra door in the bedroom interferes with its tranquillity and a view into an en suite is rarely romantic. Have as many bathrooms, shower rooms and wet rooms as you need. Make them as wonderful as you can. But unless you have enough space to place the en suite door outside the main sleeping area, think twice.

Maybe you are not currently 'a couple' but are ready to invite a long term lover into your life. Your bedroom can set the mood. First let go of everything that recalls previous affairs. This could be the time for a new mattress, new bed linen, perhaps a whole new look. Think romantic. Think sensual. Think intimate. Arrange the room as though he/she is already there, with space ready and waiting for their belongings. (Life abhors a void so it will soon be filled).

Your bedroom can be just as easily a handicap in the romantic stakes. Ready for him? Then ban images of single women, teddy bears and too many cushions on the bed which shout: "Taken". Ready for her? This is the bedroom not Mission Control. Bar electronic gear, exercise equipment, tennis rackets and all similar bedroom turn-offs.

Children's bedrooms should be calm and cosy. The child must feel very safe. Colours need to be soft and warm. Avoid anything harsh and bright. It is a mistake to use strong primary colours as they over-stimulate and promote a hyperactive atmosphere, not one to snuggle down in. Provide adequate storage to avoid troubling clutter. *(Bibliography: Baniel. Fisher et al)* During the day children's bedrooms can be multi-functional but at night they must revert to being simple bedrooms, conducive to rest and sleep. Teenagers' rooms are personal territory and need to be respected as such.

The bedroom is the 'Room of the Bed'. It is most serene when the bed dominates and there is little else of a practical nature. If you have space, store clothes elsewhere. Your bed, bedside tables, lamps and maybe a couple of comfy chairs are all that are really needed in the way of major furnishings. Let the bed rule and the room be devoted to the five senses.

As for some secrets of the bed itself; place it in the 'command position' with a wall behind and a view of the door. Have a headboard. The wall, strengthened by a solid headboard, gives a sense of security. Windows behind the bed are at odds with this. If unavoidable, ensure heavy curtaining or shutters. The best place for a bed is facing, but not directly in line with, the door. 'Directly opposite the door' is the 'carried out feet first' position with its associated negative connotations. If this is the only option, ensure a substantial footboard and/or place furniture between the bed and door.

Should you have a very large bed with twin zipped mattresses, here is a wisdom trick from feng shui. Such beds are designed to be cobbled together and to separate. These are subtle messages you do not need. What you do is simple. With focussed intention, you strap the two mattresses together with red cloth. The binding is always red; the feng shui colour of good fortune, the Western colour of passion.

Beams are difficult. In feng shui a beam lengthways over the centre of the bed is said to divide a couple in the same way as the twin mattresses of a large bed that has not yet had the red ribbon treatment. Beams cutting across horizontally are seen as harmful to the health of anybody habitually sleeping there, with a tendency to affect the body at the level where the beam crosses. Best not risk it. Cover the beams if possible or sleep elsewhere. Otherwise, even today, a four-poster may be the answer.

The view from your bed is the last thing you see at night and the first thing each morning. It's important. Make it beautiful. For partners it should not only be pleasing but the same, so each shares the same first-and-last-thing view, a shared view on life as it were. Split views are undesirable anywhere but especially as the view from your bed.

Some are curious about the ideal direction in which to sleep. One guideline suggests that this depends on your needs at the time but, all being equal, sleeping with your head to the north is best.

Sleeping

Head North: Enhances physical wellbeing, health and vitality.

Head South: Enhances intuition and stimulates dream recall and memory.

Head East: Speeds life up (good for depression and sluggishness). Great when planning new projects and getting them off the ground.

Head West: Slows life down (good for stress, hyperactivity, restlessness and insomnia). Perfect for times of completion of projects and inner transformation.

Head North/West, South/East etc: Blends the qualities.

Your bedroom is your place to reflect and rejuvenate. It is your refuge, your oasis. In your bedroom you can be your most vulnerable self, dream your innermost dreams, abandon yourself to whatever sweet delights.

Your bedroom is sanctuary and sacred retreat. Give yourself the bedroom you deserve.

Notes

1. For a calm bedroom and peaceful sleep, make sure the space under the bed is clear, that is free from storage items and clutter.

2. Warm light is much kinder in the bedroom than the astringent 'blue' light from LEDs and electronic equipment. Numerous websites detail the possible harmful effects of blue/white LED lighting at night, including disturbance of sleep patterns, weight gain and potential links to cancer, especially breast cancer (including increased resistance to tamoxifen, a drug used to treat it). Earth Island Institute for example, states: 'Unfortunately, exposure to blue-rich light at night can lead to decreased melatonin secretion in humans. Melatonin is a hormone secreted at night by the pineal gland that helps balance the reproductive, thyroid and adrenal hormones and regulates the body's circadian rhythm of sleeping and waking.' *www.earthisland.org*

Cubby Hole

Storage areas, spaces under stairs, lofts, cellars, laundry rooms, back entrances, connecting areas, cupboards, odd-shaped spaces ... are these as beautiful as your living room? Too often they are the 'forgotten' places, the dumping grounds. A key concept of feng shui is that of the 'bagua', an energy map or diagram relating to the ground floor of any structure. The bagua represents every conceivable area of life. Lay it over the plan of your home and you can see immediately and precisely which area correlates with your money, career, health, love life, children, reputation, travel, study, creativity, happy coincidences etc. In relation to your home you can think of it as the building equivalent of an acupuncture chart. Whatever life issue you think of, it is represented in the bagua map and inescapably located in your home. It may sound far-fetched but the extent to which this is borne out in practice is astonishing. For example, a dark messy area in the love section of a home correlates all too frequently with a messed up romantic life. This means every room, every tiny space, is of equal importance. The vitality or otherwise of each area has an effect on us and those effects can be very specific. Maybe this seems a little esoteric but, even in ordinary terms, every cranny is significant to the overall feel of your home. *(For information on the bagua, see Bibliography: Collins)*.

Take a utility/laundry area. Frequently it is considered a non-room and is cluttered and unbeautiful. But a laundry room should be as pleasant as every other room. The space must be functional but can still be uplifting. If you choose, you can be a bit more playful, perhaps a little wilder or more whimsical than in the main living areas. You can experiment with colour or create a 'gallery' with posters, photographs, collages, mementos and feel-good items that don't fit easily elsewhere. And so with any 'lost' space, however small. In the laundry example, the ironing board (as every workstation) needs to be in the 'command position' or 'power spot'. If the utility area also serves as a back entrance it should greet you, like all entrances, with warmth and welcome every time you come home. Unless doing the washing is your passion, find some way of screening the appliances when not in use so your homecoming is free and light and not burdened with a heavy sense of work to be done. Equally your leaving should be a pressing invitation to return rather than a last glance at piles of work waiting for you.

Passageways too can feel neglected and unacknowledged. I recall a long, low, old thick-walled cottage, a wonderful place with distant upland views, the sort of spot where you want to pick up the binoculars. Red kites circle the garden, swoop down for the hunks of meat on the outsize bird table and come to rest in the trees. I saw the house shortly after friends moved in. It was cosy and inviting with a roaring Christmas fire but marred upstairs (as the new owners recognised) by a long narrow tunnel of a landing. Now the landing is a vital living space. You no longer notice the length as it is broken up with bookshelves, paintings, personal treasures, a chair, a small table. It has become a place to linger awhile and mooch. My friends have made a positive out of a negative. And that's the thing to do with houses and with life.

Honour the odd spaces and treat them like any room in your home. As a child did you ever feel a tiny bit scared in a part of your home or someone else's? Use your inner child sensitivity to unearth those places where the energy is depleted, the unloved areas, the neglected areas, the 'dead' areas, the drab attics, the dank basements. How can you heal them? The first priority is to clear and clean them. Maybe a colour makeover would help. Certainly good light works wonders anywhere, any time. Unused or empty rooms, as much as cluttered corners, can feel creepy as their energy becomes depleted. We need to bring life to them any way we can; by entering them, placing flowers there, switching on the radio, opening windows and so on.

Each area, however seemingly insignificant, adds to the whole and impacts on us constantly. We need to invite *all* the odd corners fully into our home.

Garage

The garage and other outhouses are often the greatest culprits in the saga of the unloved space, but as for every corner within the house, they should be uncluttered, ordered and pleasant.

Before cars, people had horses and carriages, ponies and traps, donkeys and carts. The buildings in which these were stabled were set apart from the house for obvious reasons. The car is the descendant of them all and the garage is the new coach house. As part of their heritage from that earlier time, garage walls are frequently left in a rough unfinished state inside. Unfortunately the modern materials are rarely so congenial.

Detached garages are still the best option. The reasons are many. Attached garages often occupy a favoured position with two, sometimes even three, outside walls. Do you really need that space as a garage? Might it not be more agreeable as living space, allowing light from more than one direction, precious multi-aspect sunshine, into your home? The comings and goings, the noise, the restless energy of the car and the garage activities detract from the tranquillity of the home and especially from those rooms adjacent to or above the garage. Those houses where an attached garage juts out in front are 'garage dominated' and the occupants, as feng shui tells us, can complain of stress. They are often, as it were, 'driven'. Better no garage at all. And, crucially, when a garage is attached, fumes can penetrate adjoining walls and seep through ceilings into upstairs rooms. However slight the seepage at any one moment, when constant the effects are cumulative. Leaving the car outside is better for health (and some say better for the car).

Rooms over garages feel unstable. Areas over any empty space are best for storage or bathrooms or at a push, for creative activities, work etc. Such bedrooms for instance, are undesirable as they are not conducive to restful sleep. Respect the old adage: 'Don't sleep over a void'. If you do have rooms over empty areas, they need 'anchoring'. For this, feng shui uses heavy objects, square shapes, yellows and earth shades. Large low comfortable well-padded furniture, dark floors, thick rugs and heavy terracotta pots will help stabilise a too-spacey feel. Lingam stones are outstanding for grounding energy. Or, you can devise symbolic fixes (laced with strong intention) such as blown-up images of trees, since trees are so deeply rooted.

Ideally the garage door is hidden from the front entrance. The larger the door, the more it grabs attention. Garage doors are huge. When front door and garage door compete, the garage wins suggesting that the car is more important than the people. Where a garage door does dominate, the front door should be enhanced to attract the eye and/or the garage door made as unobtrusive as possible by, for example, being painted the same colour as its surroundings

Garage problems are compounded when the garage is a mess. We need to retrieve the garage, think of it as the car room and enhance it with the same loving care as any other part of the home. This is particularly important when the garage is attached and used as a secondary entrance to the house.

Even the garage should raise, rather than deplete, your energy.

Garden

Since the Garden of Eden, we human beings have found refreshment, solace and pleasure in gardens. Now, more than ever in our increasingly pressurised urban lifestyles, gardens are vital for they re-connect us with the cycles of nature.

As we pass from any one place to another, our anticipation is heightened by its threshold (or otherwise by its lack). A Special Entrance into the garden always makes magic. You are entering sacred territory. The entrance may be classical, rustic or contemporary as appropriate.

If the garden is large, it may benefit from having more than one threshold into its different spaces, each framing its own view. The space can be subdivided with hedging or other means to create 'gardens within gardens'. Always and everywhere quality is more important than quantity. Tiny gardens and patios can make wonderful outdoor 'rooms'. Glimpsed 'views beyond' give an illusion of infinity. Water, however small a feature, is wonderful for its reflective qualities in both senses of the word. Walls painted white 'expand' the area. A 'white garden', all silvery leaves and white night-scented flowers shimmering in the moonlight, is mesmerising. Walls and corners define the limit of any space so, if concealed by planting, even a miniature garden can seem limitless.

A back garden works best when 'contained', allowing a sense of security and privacy. Such a garden is a world apart, a haven allowing us to be out in the open yet buffered from the world. A secluded garden is one we will use. Equally important are ways in and out, otherwise there can be a dead-end sense of congestion. Crucially a rear garden that slopes down from the house (with no feng shui 'mountain behind') can feel unstable in the same way, and with the same effects, as a steep staircase tumbling to the front door. It needs some protective height from hedges, banks or summerhouses etc. to counteract the falling away.

An excessively yang environment, most starkly seen in newly built housing estates with their straight lines, sharp angles and harsh landscaping, can be transformed with a few yin features such as meandering paths, changes of direction, spirals or different levels. Straight-edged paving is softened instantly with greenery spilling over the hard edges. If, on the contrary, an outside area is too fussy (yin), hard (yang) landscaping can give it definition and interest.

Water is entrancing in a garden. Points to consider are that moving water either flows towards the house or radiates in a 360° formation as in some fountains. Standing behind a fountain with water jetting away from you is the water equivalent of someone turning their back on you. It doesn't feel good. Water flowing towards a building energises it. Flowing away, it weakens it.

L-shaped and other non-rectangular houses can be strangely unsettling. This sense is profoundly unconscious but human beings originally lived in houses which were 'whole' in shape – circular, square, oblong – and whole seems to be what we are most aligned with. Feng shui is uneasy with asymmetry and offers simple and aesthetically pleasing solutions to contain it. It does this by visually 'enlarging' the ground plan of the house into an imaginary rectangle, squaring it off, as it were, to reincorporate the 'missing' parts of the building. The 'incomplete area' left by an L-shaped or other lopsided house can be filled in with a conservatory or veranda. Or, more simply … fences, low walls, hedges, flower beds, lighting, even a difference in paving, can square it off. Another way is to 'mark' a 'missing corner' with, say, a tree or boulder. Subtle though they are, these devices add enormously to the feel-good of both house and garden. There is, admittedly, some ambiguity here. Rectangularity is not essential for visual appeal. Irregular shapes can be beguiling but usually, even the most beautiful are more satisfying when there is some suggestion of 'squaring off' in the landscaping. In the hands of a master architect, of course, buildings can curve and wind and undulate and draw you in and entice you on and be extraordinarily nourishing. *(Bibliography: Day)* For the most part, however, unless the architecture is outstanding, houses offering at least some gesture towards rectangularity sustain us most.

A garden can double as security system with beautiful but barbed plants and prickly hedges such as holly. Crunchy gravel lets you hear people approaching. Good lighting deters anyone with nefarious intent. Together they are as effective as any burglar alarm – and prettier.

We can create delight even in the most lifeless of surroundings. Seating under a tree or benches at a garden table invite us to linger and enjoy; barbecues and outdoor fires are wholly pleasurable, possibly because they reconnect us with our ancient origins; lighting adds mystery and promotes safety; paths which curve or contain some change of direction can, if they allow space for two people to walk side by side, add a dreamlike quality. Statuary and garden art, arbours and arches, sundials, weathervanes, earthenware pots and reflective objects can punctuate, highlight and direct attention. A 'secret' garden. A pond. Half-hidden views. All these are deeply romantic and nourishing. Summerhouses and hideaways add enormously to enchantment (and market value). They are all the more entrancing if in complete contrast (mood/style etc.) to your home. If there is enough space for them to be fenced off in a little garden of their own, then we have perfection. A lovely balcony or even a window box, however, will nurture the property more than acres of uncared-for land.

Plants align us with the seasons. Fragrance, herbs and texture beguile our senses. Our own organic vegetables nourish us like no shop-bought fare. We can invite wild-life (and add to our delight) by planting shrubs and flowers that attract bees, butterflies and birds. Water encourages frogs and dragonflies. Importantly we should leave a wild place at the bottom of the garden, quite undisturbed, for the fairies, the 'devas' of the earth. (It has even been spoken that eating a wild primrose helps us see a fairy). More prosaically, wildflowers help conservation. By providing bird baths, birdhouses, feeders, butterfly habitats, water bowls and so on, we lure in beautiful creatures of the wild. Red squirrels, garden birds, hedgehogs! For me they were supreme early morning moments when a roe deer occasionally honoured me with her presence, standing motionless at the bottom of the garden like some shining mythical unicorn.

Above all, gardens restore a sense of tranquillity which, so often and for so many, is hard to find in the hectic 21st century.

Notes

Even tiny plots can be havens of biodiversity and, through our gardens, together we can make a significant contribution towards the healing of our much abused planet:

1. **Flood**

   Concreting and tarmac over large swathes of land augment (and cause) flooding. We need to allow good drainage on *our* land by, for example, using porous landscaping materials such as gravel; designing paths of 'stepping stone' flags; laying paving stones checkerboard-style with alternate 'green' squares; edging pavers individually with say, aromatic chamomile lawn turf etc. More ambitiously, we might create a 'rain garden'.

2. **Drought**

   We can collect water from guttering etc. into water butts for use at times of scarcity. We can recycle waste water with grey water systems. We could even bring back the dew ponds, those beautiful, mysterious, evocative, sometimes ancient, small saucer-shaped pools which retain a constant supply of fresh water. They are now largely destroyed but once featured widely in our landscape.

3. Chemical fertilisers and pest control

Chemicals poured onto land (and leached into streams and rivers and ultimately the seas) poison wildlife, kill pollinating insects and reduce the vitality of food. Let our own flowers and vegetables be grown organically, bio-dynamically and/or with methods such as methods such as permaculture. We can ban the chemicals at least from our own small corner of God's earth.

4. Maximising a small vegetable patch

If land is limited and you wish to grow more, use less seed and dramatically reduce workload investigate, for example, raised bed metre-square gardening. (*Bibliography: Bartholomew. Dunford*) Growing herbs, fruit and vegetables in pots can also be highly productive – and beautiful. (*Bibliography: Maguire*)

5. Alternative technology

Awareness of this developing field can help us help our gardens (and homes) which in turn can help the wider environment. A fantastic place for advice (and a wonderful day out) is the Centre of Alternative Technology at Machynlleth in West Wales. *www.cat.org.uk*

See Bibliography for information on some of the above suggestions.

Sanctuary

Fire

Hearth and home. For the Ancient Greeks the two were synonymous. For us too on a cold winter's night the fire, if we are lucky enough to have one, is indeed the heart of our home. Houses without a fireplace, we say, have no focal point. 'Focus' is in fact the Latin for 'hearth'.

From prehistory fire has represented comfort and security. For our earliest ancestors the fire warmed them, cooked their food, provided light on dark nights and scared away hungry predators. Our forebears could come together in peace and safety in the glow of the fire after unimaginably hard days. This sense is encoded deep within us and our celebration of fire has persisted in fire festivals around the world. A highlight of my own life remains my first bonfire as a child. It was a simple local affair with chestnuts roasting and potatoes baking slowly in the embers. Even the fairy lights in the trees were fire, lighted candles in jam jars covered with brightly coloured crepe paper. In those days I used to visit a house where plaited loaves were left to rise on the hearth and at Christmas, the tree was lit with real candles. Such delights.

There is something mysterious about fire. We could, right now, rub two sticks together and create a flame and make a fire and from that fire light another and still another and that fire could be kept alight, passed from place to place for evermore. The eternal flame. Life eternal.

In ancient Greece there was such a custom. The bride's mother would take a flame from her own ever-burning fire and, carrying the flaming torch aloft, lead the wedding party to the home-to-be of the new couple and light their fire from it. It was only then that their house became a home. Their dwelling received the soul of home, the soul of Hestia.

Hestia was goddess of home, hearth, hospitality and of fires and flames everywhere. She presided over domestic life. Every home had a round hearth dedicated to her at the centre of the house, its fire tended by the virgin daughters of the household. Each meal began and ended with a prayer to Hestia and to secure her blessing, infants were carried in a circle around the hearth, the altar of Hestia, as part of their naming ceremony. Uniquely there are no statues of her as she, this gentlest and most revered deity of the ancient pantheon, could only be seen in the flicker of the flames. Her name signifies 'Essence'. She is the spirit, the core, the true nature, the centre of things. Her emblems are the flame and the circle. The goddess and the fire. The Spirit of the Home.

By extension, Hestia was the goddess of architecture. Houses, she intimated, should be built from the midpoint out with the hearth and its sacred flame at the centre. Hestia was also guardian of the city and indeed the world. A public hearth, the Prytaneion, was consecrated to her. Flame was taken from this fire and carried to the colonies and smaller settlements to be kept alight there. Thus, through the living flame, the far-flung populations maintained the bond with the mother city. This is the origin of the Olympic flame which is still carried to the Games from ancient Olympia. The source of Hestia's fire was the conflagration raging at the centre of the earth, connected by umbilical cord to the 'navel stone' or 'Omphalos' in Delphi which marked the Axis Mundi, the centre of the universe. The fire was synonymous with the centre. Vesta was Hestia's Roman counterpart and the only circular temple in the Roman Forum was dedicated to Vesta. There too burned a perpetual fire tended by priestesses, the Vestal Virgins. Classical architecture was thus linked with the centrality of the hearth and its fire.

Whilst the fireplace is rarely at the physical centre nowadays, the hearth, when present, remains the emotional heart of the home and a lighted fire never fails to symbolise comfort and security. We can add to its enchantment by becoming acquainted with the differing qualities of firewood and by burning aromatic fruitwoods such as pear, apple or cherry. We can throw on orange peel, rosemary or cinnamon. When there is no fire blazing, remember not to leave a dark gaping hole which drains rather than radiates energy. Give the fireplace some other role. Make it come alive with flowers, lighted candles, incense, pine cones, foliage or find some other way to keep it as a living symbol of warmth and welcome throughout the year.

Even without a fireplace each room needs a focal point. We are drawn to flame, light and movement (a flickering fire has all three) so where there is no fireplace, take extra care to make the most of other light sources; windows in the daytime, electric lighting and candlelight at nightfall. The television so easily becomes the focus of attention but rooms are more congenial when the TV does not dominate. The market itself is finding ingenious ways of hiding and revealing the television. Now it's here, now it's not. Secondary focal points can add interest although these are usually best away from a diagonal placement in the corners where they can feel somewhat unsettling.

Now, unseasonably, it is snowing. A springtime blizzard has descended and the house where I am has no fire. Oh how seductive friends' homes where there is a real fire. How I am drawn to visit those friends. How hard to drag myself away. How snug and comfy their homes.

And it is not only the flames. The chimney itself allows a healthy, pleasant and almost palpable air exchange which allows the building to 'breathe' and 'live'.

Fire is in our human DNA. Learning to harness fire (along with a very small list of other special qualities) ultimately made possible the staggering human civilisations this earth has been home to, right up to our own astounding, rapidly evolving culture which forever bears the imprint of all that went before. Consequently there is nothing that gives us such contentment as a real fire.

Notes

1. **Fire: the research**

   Research indicates consistently that when we are in front of an open fire we are more relaxed, bond with one another more easily and our blood pressure drops significantly. Remarkably it doesn't even have to be the real thing. A video of flickering flames with the crackling sound of burning logs will do. (*Bibliography: Lynn*) There is an app for everything and if you do not have a fireplace you can simulate a real fire through your smartphone. My friend's yappy, excitable little dog calms down instantly when the 'fire' is blazing and crackling on the television.

2. Making it easy

If dust, work and the ongoing cost of a fire put you off, think again. Technology has come to the rescue. Today's most innovative log burners greatly minimise these problems and are much more efficient than traditional open fires. Stoves contain the fire behind glass doors but when you want to heighten the comfort, flicker, crackle and aroma, just open the doors. Glass doors are also available for fitting to conventional fireplaces.

3. Keeping it environmentally friendly

The latest log burners are not only highly efficient and economical but timber is said by most authorities to be as environmentally friendly as we can get since the CO_2 emitted from the burning logs is only equal to the CO_2 absorbed by the tree when growing. Woodburners are thus potentially carbon neutral. Opinion is mixed but see information from The Wood Heat Organization at *www. woodheat.org/wood-burning-and-the-environment.html*

4. **Centrality of the hearth**

    Maybe the Ancient Greeks were onto something. A chimney at the centre of the house warms more of the house with less cost, less effort and less fuel. *(Bibliography: Day. 2015)*

5. **Hestia/Vesta counterparts**

    Brigid: Celtic goddess of all things fiery; flame, light, candles, warmth, heat, forges, sunrise, the hearth. Priestesses tended an everlasting fire in her honour.

    Saint Brigit of Kildare: The Christianised embodiment of the goddess. Her nuns continued to keep alive the sacred fire.

    Hestia, Brigid and Saint Brigit are 'guardian of the home' archetypes invoked traditionally for their blessing. Today we can still draw on archetypal energies from myth, legend and history in order to enhance our lives (and in this case our homes).

and to light your fire ...

Beechwood fires are bright and clear
if the logs are kept a year.
Chestnut's only good, they say,
if for logs 'tis laid away.
Make a fire of Elder tree,
death within your house will be.
But Ash new or Ash old,
is fit for a queen with crown of gold.

Birch and Fir logs burn too fast,
blaze up bright and do not last.
It is by the Irish said
Hawthorn bakes the sweetest bread.

Elm wood burns like churchyard mould,
e'en the very flames are cold.
But Ash green or Ash brown
is fit for a queen with golden crown.

Poplar gives a bitter smoke,
fills your eyes and makes you choke.
Apple wood will scent your room.
Pear wood smells like flowers in bloom.
Oaken logs, if dry and old,
keep away the winter's cold.
But Ash wet or Ash dry
a king shall warm his slippers by.

—*Traditional English*

Blessing

A house warming party, if you have ever held one, proclaims to the world that you are here to stay, for a while at least in these days of high mobility. When your friends and family have celebrated with you, this house will truly be your home. A house warming is an honouring of the Spirit of the Home as a living being who will protect and nurture you and make your house a home.

There are infinite ways to bless a home. When you name a house or give it a new coat of paint or add flowers or entertain friends, you are honouring the Spirit of your Home.

Once l invited a priest-friend to bless a house that felt eerily disturbed. It was a traditional and beautiful little ceremony and seemed to change the atmosphere and in remarkable ways. The light bulbs for instance, had been fusing constantly, sometimes even exploding. After the blessing, the electricity like much else settled down and a calm fell upon the house. There are many home blessing rituals from around the world to choose from or you can create your own. You can invite someone else to act as celebrant or you yourself can invoke the blessing – with your partner, your family, your friends or alone. You may find the following structure useful.

First designate a 'Sacred Centre'. Choose the spot. Place a large candle there (matches and wax tapers close by) and, with total 'focus', declare it the Centre. To energise it, make it beautiful with 'fruits of nature' and/ or items of personal significance. Place a special stone there, your own 'omphalos'. The best home omphalos is a lingam stone since lingams have an unparalleled capacity to focus and ground energy. Meteorites, haematite or obsidian can be substituted for a lingam. But any stone will do. (Do not use a cut-glass crystal as these radiate rather than focus energy). Burn some incense if you wish.

Stand in your main entrance for a moment. Pause. Breathe. Smile. From there slowly approach the 'centre'. In your own time, light the candle taking flame from the hearth if the fire is lit. Dedicate the flame to the Guardian of the Home, however you wish to perceive her. Ask her blessing to make your home a place of sanctuary, safety and sustenance for all who dwell there and all who visit. Request that her fire may ever grant light, warmth, nourishment and comfort. Each person present can make their own candle dedication, silently or aloud.

For a more elaborate blessing, create a subsidiary altar in each area of your home. This can be as simple as a small table, shelf or stool covered with a beautiful cloth. Place flowers, votive candles and items pertaining to your life or the room. If you have a garden you may wish to create an outside shrine too. Taking the flame from the mother candle, your large central candle, light each candle in turn making a dedication appropriate to the room (for nourishment in the kitchen, rest and refreshment in a bedroom, creative inspiration in a studio and so on). Then light the garden candle and walk around the property invoking blessings on your home. Re-cross the threshold. Pause there awhile. Return to the Centre where you began. Give thanks, knowing your home is blessed. And find contentment there. Finally, as with all ritual, finish with a celebration; a meal, a glass of wine, a group hug, dancing the night away or with some quiet music, whatever feels appropriate right now.

The blessing of a house is a lovely rite of passage and one you can repeat any time you wish to re-dedicate your home. There are myriad ways to do it. If you wish to design your own ceremony, the above can serve as a model.

Notes

In any candle dedication:

1. The point of power is the moment of ignition.
2. Your intention is released into the cosmos the instant the flame is extinguished.

Caution

Never play with fire. Give it due respect and adhere to the normal safety precautions. A good way of carrying flame is with a small lighted candle in a fireproof holder with a wide base or in a proper 'Wee Willie Winkie light your way to bed' candlestick. Beeswax candles are the most evocative of all but need extra care as beeswax burns hotter and its molten wax can scald. Sand and water are candle safety measures. Churches often use sand under their votive candle stands whilst candles floating in water are always magical.

Some ceremonies for making your home special

1. 'Space clearing' your home when you move in, at times of change and upheaval or whenever you wish to refresh or cleanse the atmosphere. *(For space clearing see Bibliography: Kingston; Linn)*

2. A house warming in a new house or one you have just refurbished.

3. Saying goodbye and thanking your home when you leave, consciously withdrawing your energy. This way you are not energetically 'split' and the new occupants are able to start afresh without running on your residual energy.

Sacred Space

There is a place on the cliffs high above the sea. Tiny islands, just a few minutes' boat trip away, appear as if newly birthed from the ocean only, you feel sure, to sink back into its depths the moment you look away. Sometimes the sea is calm and of the deepest cerulean blue. At other times it is grey, savage, colourless, flinging itself against the rocks way below. But up here, you are in the sky, above it all … you, the ravens and the peregrines. Still you remain a creature of the earth, your bare feet firmly on the ground, caressed by a myriad wild flowers. This light is like no other. Everything takes on a different aspect as if seen through a veil. The sun is soft, its shadows indigo. Artists flock here, captivated by the strange and beautiful light. For me it has always been a place of mystery and magic inhabited by buzzards and seals and the ghosts of saints.

You pick your way through ancient Celtic ruins. You place a few cowslips on the wayside shrine, linger by the healing well, dip your hands in its waters, dip your feet in the wild watercress close by. Climbing further you come upon a miniature, cliff-top chapel only 12ft (around 3.5m) wide inside. You enter and immerse yourself in its peace, You lose track of time. You light a candle. Sit. Kneel. Say a prayer. Meditate. Contemplate. Cross yourself with the holy water, that lovely Christian (though universal) gesture linking your chakras – third eye, heart and thymus; the vertical and horizontal forces; the yin and yang, the male and female within you. You leave, uplifted and changed.

When I lived in this mystical landscape, I was drawn like a pilgrim to the little chapel. Many of us have such places, often in nature, which soothe our soul.

Perhaps there is some universal need for 'sanctuary' for it would seem that, down the aeons, people have fashioned places and ritual spaces where they could reach 'beyond'. The earliest sanctuaries were often circular and open air. Later they tended to be rectangular; temples and synagogues, basilicas and churches, mosques and chapels. Following disaster we often consecrate a shrine to cleanse and sanctify the land, honour those caught in its tragedies and offer solace to those left behind. But one way or another, for one reason or another, human beings have always created spaces dedicated to sanctuary.

Each is unique; governed by the terrain, the space available and the cultural context of its creators. So what makes sanctuary? What are the prerequisites common to all? They are few, simple and powerful … path, periphery, portal, place and peace … a mini-pilgrimage, there and back; into profundity and back to the 'world' enriched in some unquantifiable way. My little chapel is classic … you follow the trail. You enter the tranquillity, You retrace your steps as with a benediction.

The *path* represents the 'way', the 'journey'. The *periphery* is container for the safe space within. This boundary need not be 'solid'. The stone circles and sacred groves of antiquity did not have continuous edges. Their margins were 'permeable', fractal in nature with breathing spaces between. The *portal* is the entrance, the threshold you must cross. Path, periphery and portal slow you down, set the mood and heighten the experience. The *place* is the sanctuary enclosure itself. It offers calm for your mind and balm for your soul … *peace*.

In the previous chapter we spoke of having a 'sacred centre'. We can elaborate on this if we wish and create a dedicated home sanctuary.

Size, shape and placing matter not. Your sanctuary can be inside or out, personal space or for sharing, an entire room or a chair in a quiet corner. A garden hideaway may make the perfect 'poustinia' *[from the Russian for 'desert'],* a simple space for silence and prayer. At home, the area available is often restricted so some of the preconditions may be symbolic. A floorboard over which you step may act as portal and so on.

The space might exist already, perfect as it is right now and needing no adornment. Your awareness of its special nature is all that is required. Alternatively you may enjoy designing somewhere wholly new. Your sanctuary can be almost stark in its simplicity, maybe with one arresting image or a single candle or you may wish to embellish it more extravagantly. The choices are yours.

So what to bring to your sanctuary? There is no one way. There are, however, numerous traditions to turn to for inspiration. Frequently, one's own native heritage offers a deep – maybe the deepest – well of meaning and inspiration, even if the underlying beliefs are questioned or rejected. If you have a particularly strong faith, you can still adopt and adapt customs you like from other cultures. Perhaps, for instance, taking off your shoes is not part of your tradition but you may choose to do this when entering your sanctuary. A home altar provides a focus for your cherished objects. Flowers and lighted candles are universal. symbols of peace. You can give thanks for the bounty of the earth by introducing 'objects of nature', foliage and fruits of the harvest. Water plays a part in most sanctuary traditions. It calms. It refreshes. It is the first requirement of life and its symbolism is vast. A bowl of fresh water or perhaps water from a special river or spring, can be 'blessed' with a prayer or in some way of your own. You may like to dedicate it as a pebble pool, adding special pebbles to represent your prayers. (Refresh the water often). The burning of incense in sanctuary spaces is at least 4000 years old as we know from records dating back to ancient Egypt and China and it has ritual and symbolic significance in most major religions. Aromatic herbs, aromatherapy oils and fragrant blossom are also potent mood-enhancers. (*Bibliography: Hirsch*) A few personal treasures placed on the altar can represent an 'offering'. Some traditions make much of honouring the ancestors. You can, for example, gather together in a beautiful box or bag a few mementos of those beloveds who have gone before … a book, a ring, a photo. Perennial plants, say lilies of the valley, can be grown outside to bloom again, year by year in remembrance. A 'healing tree' (or branch) on which to attach prayers, hopes and dreams is a very old practice. Whilst inner silence is the ultimate gift of sanctuary, certain music calms us, particularly some sacred and classical music. This is especially true, it is now understood, of slow music with a repetitive 10-second cycle (such as much of Verdi) since this matches the body's natural 10-second cardiovascular waves. (*Bibliography: Sleight*) Birdsong quietens the spirit. Bells, gongs and singing bowls chosen for the beauty of their tone find their way into many traditional sanctuary spaces. The elemental whispers from wind chimes and Aeolian harps echo, as it were, the sound of silence. Sanctuary, however, goes further. In replenishing you, it enables you more easily to give back to the world. As a practical symbol of this you may consider an 'offertory box' for spare coins or even for the tithing of a regular amount.

Visually a sanctuary space needs to be free from unnecessary distraction. Generally it is best when walls are white or a calm neutral shade and the flooring is simple. You may wish to counterbalance this with colour and it can be rewarding to explore the time-honoured colours associated with the festivals of the liturgical year of a chosen religion or, perhaps, those linked with the old Celtic 8-fold 'wheel of the year' which demarcates the turning of the seasons through the solstices, equinoxes and midpoints. Calligraphy, icons, sacred imagery, symbols, collages, embroideries, ceramics, paintings and sculpture on the walls or in niches may focus attention. Old timber can help impart a sense of timelessness. Stained glass filtering the light through windows is hugely atmospheric and small antique pieces can sometimes be picked up quite cheaply. It can be fun to browse junk shops and reclamation yards for appropriate items that 'speak' to you. Treat them all with reverence. But always ... less is better than more.

Sanctuary of course is to be found anywhere, sometimes in the most unexpected of places. It can be private or public, indoors or out, intentional or 'given'. Wherever you recognise the ineffable, sanctuary is there. Ultimately, of course, sanctuary is within and available any time, any place. It is the 'still small centre', the 'grace' which spills out and blesses all it touches.

Notes

The 'Quiet Garden Movement' and the 'labyrinth' are increasingly popular sanctuary-related resources.

1. The first Quiet Garden opened in England in 1992, the vision of an Anglican priest, Philip Roderick. The movement has since spread worldwide. Members open their homes and gardens from time to time, offering hospitality and spiritual renewal. Each is different. There may, for example, be a semi-structured programme with a guest facilitator, perhaps a family friend, interspersed with quiet times of solitude in the garden or inside followed by a shared meal. Quiet Gardens are appearing now in public spaces; inner city areas, schools, hospitals and, more recently, prisons.

2. Labyrinth rock carvings date back to Neolithic times. Their original purpose is a mystery but they have reappeared throughout history, the best

known perhaps being the medieval floor labyrinths of French cathedrals, most notably in Chartres. Today there is a labyrinth resurgence with people all over the world 'walking the labyrinth' as a meditation practice. A labyrinth can be permanent with, for instance, stone or turf 'walls' or it can be canvas and portable. It can be very large allowing many people to walk it simultaneously or small enough for a private garden.

3. Peregrines. Ravens. *(page 187)* ... what synchronicity that the skies in this ancient place of pilgrimage are patrolled by these two, circling the air as guardians of this sacred site. Both species are rich in symbolism. In many cultures ravens symbolise eternal life, linking heaven and earth while peregrines portend visionary power, wisdom and guardianship. The very name 'peregrine' signifies 'pilgrim' or 'wanderer'. Melanie Reinhart writes "In the symbolic associations around the word 'peregrine', we see rich material associated with the bird, a species of falcon. The peregrine's flight reaches astonishing speed ... it is the fastest creature on earth. As a raptor, it has acute sight, even at long distance. A royal bird in ancient Egypt, its flight represents the soul soaring to the heights of mystical perception; the god Horus was depicted with a falcon's head, often with sun-disk above it" . *(Bibliography: Reinhart)*

The Big Six

1. Comfort and safety first. This includes emotional comfort and safety.

2. The front door; unmistakable, prominent, solid wood, beautiful and welcoming.

3. Multi-aspect windows in every (but the tiniest) room, in wood window frames.

4. Softened corners.

5. Your bedroom; cosy, intimate, warm and nurturing.

6. Living only with what you love and/or use.

alchemy – transformation – delight

The Dirty Dozen

Here is a checklist of some things to avoid:

1. **Art**

   Sculptures of mutilated bodies (e.g. copies of Venus de Milo etc. with no arms); troublesome images (e.g. violent, gruesome); images/photos expressing sadness, anger or fear.

Note

Original art has more vitality than copies, however lowly or great the artist.

2. **Colour**

Colours and colour schemes you don't like.

3. **Decorations and furnishings**

Old peeling discoloured wallpaper; worn, stained, tatty, threadbare furnishings; dark dingy dated décor.

4. **Hunting trophies**

Skulls; stuffed animals.

5. **Lighting**

Overly bright lighting; fluorescent lighting; harsh overhead lighting as sole source of illumination; absence of shadow.

6. **Living things**

Poorly plants; 'no longer fresh' flowers; 'unfriend-ly' plants (sharp or spiky appearance, the ones that 'bite'); old dusty dried flowers and potpourri.

7. **Mirrors**

Mirrors that diminish and distort your self-im-age; mirrors in bedrooms (unless covered during sleep); mirrors in dining rooms; mirrors reflect-ing disquieting views; mirrors hung opposite one another, reflecting each other into infinity (these disorient people and deplete environmental and personal energy).

Note

Mirrors that distort self-image include for example: dirty mirrors; foggy antique mirrors; poor quality mirrors; mirrors with unflattering lighting; mirrors at the wrong height (e.g. cutting off part of your head); mirrors that fragment images such as mirror tiles, mirrors with bevelled edges, 'window' mirrors etc.

8. Odours

Mouldy smells; smelly cat litter trays; doggy smells; synthetic scents (synthetic scented candles, potpourri, household products etc.)

9. Sounds

Sounds that grate on you (from music to noisy fridges).

10. Too much

Excess ornamentation; clutter; 'comfort stuff' (compare comfort eating).

11. Water features

Noisy electric indoor water features (keep the water feature but get the noise sorted); murky aquariums.

12. Zero tolerance

Guns, swords, spears, knives … as décor; items that are dangerous, broken, or do not work; items that let you down practically or in terms of your self-esteem; items that remind you of unhappy times; items with negative or ambivalent associations; items you find ugly; items that irritate; uPVC.

Feel-Good

These pages have all been about 'feel-good'. If it feels good, it is good. End of story. If it ain't broke don't fix it. There are so many factors, so many energies that combine to create an atmosphere. Many of these are subtle; unseen, unknown, unknowable. Most important are comfort and safety plus a subliminal feeling of comfort and safety. Otherwise there are no rules (and in any case rules are made to be broken or at the very least bent). This book is about living with what you love, not what you loved once but what you adore right now. It is about being surrounded only by that which lifts your energy in this moment. You deserve nothing less. Our identification with home is so deep that dream interpretation claims that dreams of 'house' are really dreams about oneself.

Many of us, however, are not currently living in the perfect home for our soul and don't always know the cause. We may blame the house but few houses are beyond redemption. Probably none are perfect or, if so at one moment, cease to be as life changes. These pages offer simple and mostly inexpensive ways of healing our living spaces; the discordant structural features, the unbalanced yin and yang, the lack of flow, the idiosyncratic things that serve us badly. The healing can be an incremental little by little thing. Every small adjustment can make a huge change in our contentment, the secret smile we feel when we come home. Maybe you buy a wonderful picture. It lifts your mood every time you see it. It expresses you. And the odd thing is that the more your home is an expression of you, the more others will be captivated by it. Often discarding does as much for the ambience as acquiring new. Frequently the two go together. You let go of something that's tired and miraculously the new perfect item seems to manifest. But our concern is not about 'things'. Simple flowers and candles lighten the energy as effectively. Harmony comes from living with who we are, not necessarily with what is stylish. It is not about following fashion. If we genuinely love what's 'in' right now that's great, providing we let go when our attraction to that particular style passes. Life changes and we change. Our environment needs to change with us.

There is no suggestion that every 'cure' or quick fix should, or even could, be carried out in every instance. The use of one may preclude others. Some will not be appropriate or to your taste. Think of something else to do the job. Regard them all as general principles remembering that sometimes the existing 'problem' is the best, or only, solution in the circumstances. Or you may do something deliberately which breaks the 'rules' but to stunning effect. It is about tuning into and trusting your intuition. Use only those means that blend with your current dreams and are appropriate for the space.

Whilst few, if any, houses will have all these feel-good factors, they are criteria to consider when building, moving or revamping. Since our surroundings have such a powerful effect on our deep energy (as borne out by muscle testing) there is a moral imperative on developers to consider all factors which may affect wellbeing. But, for us right now, if we haven't got them, we haven't got them, so we work around that and make our home as life-enhancing as we can in other ways.

Many concepts in this book derive from the ancient art of feng shui but all translate effortlessly to present-day lifestyles. They are timeless. The Chinese word 'ch'i' has been used repeatedly though somewhat reluctantly. We have no equivalent however. It is usually translated as 'energy' or 'life force' and is seen as the ever-changing 'charge' which animates and connects all that is. Ch'i is life itself, strong and clear or discordant and destructive, the life we share with the oceans, rocks, music, fireflies and our possessions. There is no dualism here. All is one. When one is in pain or broken, all suffer. When another is healed, all benefit. In our homes we can influence the ch'i so easily and that ripples out into the wider world in ways we will never know. As above, so below. As within, so without.

'Yin' and 'yang' are also useful in regard to our homes. Again there is no direct translation although they encompass so much. Becoming acquainted with their qualities makes it possible to see at a glance what could be added or removed to balance a space. The joy is that yin and yang offer boundless ways of doing this. Whether or not we take 'ch'i' and its 'yin/yang' aspects literally, they are exceedingly useful in helping us assess the places we inhabit so we can make them ever more congenial. In practice yin and yang allow a juxtaposition of materials, objects and textures, making for a deeply personal and tactile environment. Things that are really 'you' will meld together beautifully because they come from the same source – you.

Do not take my word for it. Check it out for yourself. Do you feel uncomfortable in a given space? If so, maybe a yin/yang count will reveal the imbalance. If you feel especially relaxed, perhaps the room has windows on two sides and is nicely proportioned. By being aware of our surroundings and armed with some simple guidelines we begin to recognise why we feel safe and content in some places and stressed in others (and what can be done about it). Thinking laterally with these tools to hand, we know that internal layout and external appearance is ever-malleable and that we can transform an uncomfortable, badly proportioned house into a gorgeous home.

The impact of our surroundings on our psyche cannot be overstated. Usually its power is unconscious but it is there constantly; holding sway over us spiritually, emotionally and practically. Today, too often, the classic paradigm (golden mean, flow, polarity and the rest) is disregarded. And we pay a heavy price. Contemporary architecture can produce the most beautiful, inspiring and satisfying spaces and this is a passionate plea to developers to rethink the mediocrity and downright ugliness which have become the accepted norm and to start planning our neighbourhoods with the eye of the artist and sensitivity of the healer. When we design our own home, the above pointers are here to guide us today, as they have always been.

For me this book is primarily about creating a sense of place. It is the magic of stepping into a new and special environment, crossing the many thresholds between outer and inner and between different spaces within. It is about balance and texture, the handmade, the 'organic', the tactile. It is about bringing life and warmth into our spaces and into our life. It is the possibility of a whole new way of seeing.

It is about kindling the fire in our hearth.
May you always have a fire glowing in your hearth.

And in your heart.

Susan x

Appendix 1:
Summaries

Feel-Good Secrets (Checklist)

Energy (ch'i)

- Benevolent location (natural or simulated)

- Harmonious placement

- Light and shade – a balance of yin and yang

- Softened corners

- Flow

- The golden mean proportion

- The fractal dimension

- Good composition

🦞 Sensitive ornament

🦞 Simplicity and lack of clutter

🦞 The X-factor

Location

🦞 Protection (height) behind, either:

   🐍 Natural (mountains, hills, woodland etc.)

   🐍 Simulated (walls, fences, hedges, earth banks, shrubs, trees, summer houses)

🦞 Protection to a lesser degree to the sides

🦞 View in front:

   🐍 Natural (open vistas, ideally sloping down to water) or

   🐍 Simulated (with for example, water in the front garden and/or some suggestion of a green buffer in front of the house)

Placement

🦞 The 'command position' or 'power spot' (protection behind, view of the door in front) all-important for major seating, workstations, beds and wherever you spend time

🦞 Empty centres of spaces

❦ 'Space between': furniture placement which allows people to negotiate their way easily around it

❦ 'Space behind': furniture set a little away from walls

❦ 'Space around': breathing space around everything from the largest piece of furniture to the smallest item

❦ Ergonomically correct, comfortable and comfortable-looking furniture

❦ Furniture to fit the space, not the space forced to fit the furniture

Light and shade

❦ The *presence* of contrast/polarity (yin & yang) in every space

❦ An appropriate *balance* of yin and yang

Corners (poison arrows & cobweb traps)

❦ Soft (i.e. not knife-edged) corners and edges

❦ 'Babyproofing' so no one bruises themselves on anything in your home

❦ Sympathetic plastering which transforms corners into things of beauty

❦ Traditional lime and clay renders, even for newbuild

Flow/circulation (inside)

- Absence of clutter
- Ease of movement (e.g. around furniture)
- Two (or more) external doors
- Doors and/or windows offset
- Doors opening into the rooms, not onto side walls
- Visual fluidity, glimpses of what lies beyond
- Layout that respects the natural energy flows:
    - Quiet rooms at the back
    - Active rooms at the front
- 'Where the eye goes, energy flows'

Flow/circulation (outside)

Space enough for two to walk right around the property

Proportion

- The golden mean (roughly 5:8) is *the* feel-good proportion ... not the only proportion that feels good but it always works
- Useful for room shapes, window sizing, garden areas, small individual objects, spacing between items etc.

Fractals

🐾 'Permeability', 'self-similarity', 'linkage' … in practice meaning a feel-good sense of flow, rhythm and cohesion (and a great sense of style)

🐾 'Views beyond'

🐾 Repeated elements and visual echoes

🐾 Harmony and integration

🐾 Vitality and 'texture'

Composition

🐾 Sensitivity to the composition of the existing building when altering or extending

🐾 Staying in harmony with the wider environment when building new

Ornament

🐾 Only decorate construction

🐾 Do not construct decoration

Simplicity & abundance

🐾 Living only with what you love, use and/or which makes you feel good

- Free from everything else; excess ornamentation, things that have had their day, items with negative/ ambivalent associations … clutter
- Good planned storage

The air we breathe

- Fresh indoor air
- House plants to purify the air and for their beauty

Space magic!

- Imaginative use of colour and of light and shade
- Old mixed with new, contemporary with antique
- Round and square used together for added impact
- Flowers, fruit, scent, music and candles
- Other delights such as mirrors, crystals, lingam stones, symbolism as appropriate for the space and according to your fancy

Thresholds

- Kerb appeal
- Front entrance unmistakeable
- Some transitional space between road and door

🐦 Path, wide enough for two, ideally curving or not too direct, leading to the door

🐦 Well lit

🐦 Rounded/softened corners and edges. (No sharp angles pointing at people)

🐦 Tranquil

🐦 Beautiful

🐦 'Greeters'

🐦 Free from clutter

🐦 Subsidiary thresholds as beautiful as the main threshold

🐦 First and last impressions memorable

Doors (in general)

🐦 Allowing easy passage

🐦 Free to open the full 180°

🐦 Interior doors of different sizes (hierarchy of scale) – living room door larger than walk-in cupboard door, parents' bedroom door larger than children's doors

Doors (front door)

🐦 *Timber* (sourced sustainably)

- Welcoming

- Prominent

- Unambiguous

- Larger than (and without competition from) other doors, especially garage doors

- Well lit

- Clearly visible

- External definition

- A well-defined path leading to it

- Strong and solid

- Classical (unless designed by a master artist/ craftsman)

- Fanlight, if present, *above* the door

- Appropriate to the house and neighbourhood

- Well maintained. Freshly painted or natural wood in good condition

- Door furniture good quality, simple and in good condition

- Doorbell which can be heard:

  - All around the property

  - By the person doing the ringing

- Numbers and names easily read from the roadside

- Bells, names, numbers, mailboxes etc. often best placed to the side

- Letterbox visible, big enough to do its work and gentle enough not to draw blood. Ideally to the side of the door, on or through a wall

- At least 6ft (about 2m) of space between door and any wall ahead of it

- Unified (not split) views ahead of door (or anywhere)

- Appropriate to the house and neighbourhood

- Front door *used*

Halls

- A calm, welcoming, transitional space between the front door and living areas

- Well proportioned

- Some clear direction, actual or subliminal, so guests know where to go

- Living rooms (or the areas you want to attract people to) emphasised

- Greeters inside as well as outside the front door

- Pleasant. This is still the sphere of first and last impressions

Windows

- *Wooden* window frames

- External definition of windows. (Internal definition from timber framing around windows also feels good)

- Golden mean proportioning

- Multi-aspect windows

- Somewhat offset rather than directly opposite each other

- Maximising daylight (for example with taller windows)

- Allowing good ventilation (preferably cross ventilation)

- Lovely view from every window:

  - Natural, or

  - Simulated (attractive window dressing)

- View of who is coming to the property but still permitting privacy within

- Window seats. They will reward you a thousand-fold

- Low windowsills

- Splayed window reveals, softly plastered. Most beautiful are the lime and clay plasters

- Style appropriate to the house and locality

Ceilings

- 🐾 Comfortable height. (Many newbuild houses are uncomfortably low)

- 🐾 Variable room heights according to room function

- 🐾 Flat and smooth

- 🐾 Free from heavy or dangerous items suspended from them

Staircases

- 🐾 Safe (and *feeling* safe)

- 🐾 Open

- 🐾 Shallow steps

- 🐾 Gentle bends

- 🐾 Wide enough to get furniture (and people) up and down

- 🐾 Conventional, not spiral

- 🐾 Free from clutter

- 🐾 Well lit

- 🐾 Non-slip treads

- 🐾 Good handrails

- 🐾 Closed risers

- 🐾 A spacious landing

- 🐾 A landing window

- Flaring a little at the bottom

- Under-stair area utilised

- Ending anywhere other than opposite the front door

Bedrooms (in general)

- Only one door (bathroom adjoining, rather than 'en suite')

- Safe, restful, serene, calm, nurturing

- Warm colours

- Warm lighting (free from flashing electronic devices and 'blue' LED light)

- Beam-free

- Mirror-free

- Equipment-free

Bedrooms (your bedroom)

- Private

- Situated at the back (or quietest) part of the house

- Blissfully dark whenever you choose, day or night

- Neither too large nor too small (intimate but not cramped)

- Equality (space, lighting etc.) the same on both sides of the bed

- Same view from both sides of the bed

- Minimal furnishings and storage units

- Containing only items you love and that support you and boost your self-image

- The whole a shrine to the senses

Beds

- In the command position:

  - Protection behind

  - View of the door in front (bed diagonally, not directly, opposite the door)

- Dominating the room

- With a head board

- Free from items stored 'out of the way' underneath

Cubby holes and all odd spaces

- As vibrant, beautiful, organised, uncluttered, pleasant and well cared for as the areas on view

- Every space a used space, nothing neglected

- Celebrated!

Garages and other outhouses

- Organised, uncluttered, pleasant and well cared for
- Detached
- Not slept above
- Garage door not competing with (nor seen at the same time as) the front door
- The 'car room' as pleasant as any other room

Gardens

- Lighting for safety and atmosphere
- Fragrance
- Balancing of awkwardly shaped buildings with simple landscaping
- Pathways which curve or change direction
- Water: flowing towards the house or in a 360° formation
- Intimation of nature
- Invitation to wildlife
- Tranquillity

Back garden

- Having ways in and out

- Secluded: 'contained' behind and to the sides by height, natural or simulated

- Half-hidden

- A special entrance creating a threshold of surprise and delight

- 'Views beyond views' or a suggestion of something beyond

Fireplaces

- A fireplace (with the fire lit or made beautiful in some other way) evoking comfort, security and 'home'

- Acting as the main focal point

- Always dominating over the television

House blessings

- Blessing your home is in itself a feel-good secret

- There are infinite ways to bless your home. Go with your intuition

Sacred Space

- A home sanctuary is very nurturing.

Appendix 2:
Shape Shifting

To Make a Space Feel Larger and Airier

We crave space … space and light. And frequently we don't have enough of either. But space costs. It is, however, possible to live wonderfully in a small space if it is properly organised. Once, seduced by the all-embracing calm of the water, I very nearly bought a canal boat, 6ft (less than 2m) wide inside. I fancied being a water gypsy, able to move on and moor somewhere different for the night. I was struck by the lifestyle of the people who currently lived on the boat. They had good jobs, ate well, wore great clothes, had computers, bicycles, new cars, all they needed, even a 'garden'. They entertained a lot and went out. They lit wood fires when the weather was cold. They had few possessions and offloaded often but they had made this home truly beautiful. Miniscule though it was, there was an overwhelming feeling of abundance and no sense at all of lack. I didn't buy the boat but I did learn that it is quality not quantity of space that counts.

So what to do with the too-small rooms, the too-yin rooms, the dark rooms, the windowless rooms, the oppressive rooms, the rooms that have tight, narrow spaces, the 'dead' areas, those places where you feel cramped, sluggish and lethargic, the areas where the energy flow is too slow, where you can't breathe?

Many of us have these problems, if not throughout our home, certainly within a part of it. Often it is not the physical size of the space that makes it feel poky but the way the space is used. It is possible, in fact, to transform almost anywhere and make it feel airier and more spacious, usually easily and often dramatically. There are three main ways. One is to play with light directly. A second way is to amplify light through reflection. The third is, simply, to think like a designer, tricking the eye into seeing things differently.

1. Direct light

Daylight is crucial always but particularly when space is limited as light helps 'expand' space. So make the most of any available natural light, if necessary by knocking through, opening up, using borrowed light. Remember though that contrast is also necessary. A space with uniform bright light is harsh, uncomfortable and devoid of atmosphere. We experience it all too often in smart new commercial and public buildings. We need something a little more subtle in our home. Shadows are a must for a sense of comfort.

The quality of daylight we receive is known to be critical for health and there is some daylight loss with double glazing, so do all you can to maximise the daylight, for health as well as ambience. *(Bibliography: Hobday)*

Notes

1. Lighting of the walls makes them seem further away (and the room bigger).

2. Lighting of the ceiling makes the room feel higher (and the room bigger).

3. Lighting of the corners blurs them (and the room feels bigger).

Here are some ways of gaining direct light which will, in every case, make a room feel more spacious:

Light from windows

❦ Dual or multi-aspect windows

❦ Taller windows and/or 'upside down living'

❦ Thin, delicate window frames/glazing bars to allow in maximum light

❦ Contemporary plain panes without glazing bars

❦ Splayed window reveals

❦ Window reveals, frames and glazing bars white or a receding colour

❦ Simple window treatments, for example:

  ❧ Curtains hung wide enough to avoid obscuring any part of the window

  ❧ Translucent curtains

  ❧ Blinds or shutters instead of curtains

  ❧ No window coverings at all

  ❧ No ornaments on windowsills. (Fresh flowers and candles in glass or reflective containers are fine)

❦ Heavy foliage outside windows pruned for maximum light advantage

❦ Conservatories

Light from the sky

When there is no possibility of adding or changing windows, daylight from the roof can have the effect of making a room seem magically lighter, larger and pleasanter:

❦ Skylights, especially over a staircase so light is thrown onto the landing and into the stairwell and space below

❦ Lantern roofs (raised glass ceilings)

❦ Sun pipes

Borrowed light

Sometimes a building allows no way of gaining extra light through windows or from the sky but it may be possible to borrow light from other rooms with, for example: glazed inner doors; stable doors; through-ways; open hatches etc.

2. Reflected light

Light-reflective surfaces help amplify light by bouncing it around, thus making dark spaces feel lighter and livelier and the room, therefore, bigger.

Colour

White reflects all colour and gives us light. Black absorbs all colour and throws us into darkness. To make a space feel more spacious therefore, think basically white and pale. The paleness promotes a wonderful feeling of calm:

- ❦ White or pale colours on large expanses such as walls, ceilings and floors (though still ensuring a warm quality of light)
- ❦ White/pale woodwork
- ❦ A touch of black or dark colour can, strangely, increase the sense of space against pale backgrounds – and add pizzazz. It also helps balance the important yin/yang dimension. (Remember the yin-yang symbol)
- ❦ Self-colour is easier on the eye in a small space (e.g. shelves to tone with wall colour)

Finishes (handles, switches, etc.)

Look for finishes made of reflective or translucent materials

Furniture

- ❦ White/pale painted furniture
- ❦ White/pale soft furnishings

Kitchens

- ❦ Contemporary gloss units
- ❦ Light-reflective worktops
- ❦ Reflective splash-backs, kick plates etc.
- ❦ 'Oil cloth' tablecloths

Mirrors

Large mirrors are marvellous for amplifying light and 'magnifying' space. (Reflect only pleasing views, never anything which agitates you)

Paintwork

Use light-reflective paints from soft sheen to gloss. Flat-matt and chalky walls are best avoided when space is at a premium however expensive the brand of paint

Surfaces

Surfaces need to be gently reflective in order to help bounce light around

3.   Thinking like a designer

Absence of clutter

🌾 Simplify and scale down

🌾 Have nothing that is not loved or used

Borrowed space/long views

Views magically augment the sense of space. If a room feels cramped, consider how you may be able to borrow space:

🐾 Leading the eye on – to the farthest corner or as far as you can go, even beyond the room. Highlight the distant point with lighting or with some eye-catching feature

🐾 Sightlines into other spaces, each with their own quality of light

🐾 Removal of doors

🐾 Partial replacement of walls with open shelving

🐾 Window boxes outside (instead of flowers on windowsills inside) to lead the gaze beyond the room

🐾 Views through windows or patio doors

🐾 Mirrors

Ceilings

There are two key points in relation to ceilings. Firstly the higher the ceiling, the larger the room feels and vice versa. Secondly ceilings have the capacity to amplify or devour light and therefore to increase or decrease the sense of space and airiness. So, to make a room feel larger and lighter, think hard about the ceiling. Aim for it to be:

🐾 White or a receding colour

🐾 Smooth

🐾 Gently reflective

🐾 Well lit

Colour

Consider white or pale shades throughout the space. (A small touch of black or a deep rich colour – or even a single dark or strongly coloured wall – may enliven a space which now feels too bland)

Corners

Rounded or softened corners are one of the most effective ways of imparting a sense of expanded space, together with a feeling of great comfort. Harsh corners define the limits of a small room too sharply, so look for ways to 'disappear' or blur them, for example:

- Lighting – up lighting in inner corners, down lighting over outer corners (arrises)
- Corners softened structurally
- Corners softly plastered
- Light foliage in or over sharp corners

Doors

- Kept open
- Removed
- Glazed (i.e. interior doors only. Exterior doors are best solid)
- Wide

- Open throughways
- Stable doors
- Double doors
- Doors opening into rooms (not onto a side wall)
- Items that block full opening of doors removed

Fabrics

Fussiness swallows up the space. To avoid being engulfed, it is often best in a small space to go for fabrics that are:

- Plain (un-patterned)
- Light-reflective
- Smooth, sleek, slinky – as appropriate for the space
- Window blinds where appropriate (instead of curtains)

Floors

The more unbroken floor and wall space visible, the larger the area feels so consider having:

- Unified flooring throughout interconnecting areas
- Floors, white or pale
- Plain floors, for example; floorboards, tiles, stone, slate, cork or plain carpet. Rugs in small spaces are often best un-patterned and/or toning with the colour of the floor

- Skirting boards the same colour as the floor to visually extend the floor

- Cupboards, chests of drawers and kitchen base units on legs (or 'floating') to allow a view of the floor beneath

Focal points

- Not too many focal points competing for attention

- Focal points kept away from corners. For a feeling of greater space, corners need to be blurred not emphasised

- Rugs can act as focal points and be very grounding

Furniture

- Less furniture

- Light furniture which you can 'see through', 'see under', 'see behind' (i.e. with open backs, on legs, on wheels etc.)

- Low furniture and storage units

- Furniture painted white or a pale colour (Scandinavian-style) or pale wood waxed to a sheen

- Straight, contemporary lines (but still comfortable and comfortable looking)

- Stacking chairs and nesting tables

Lines

- Vertical
- Straight

Ornaments

- All but the very favourite ornaments removed – ruthlessly
- One eye-catching ornament you love is more effective than numerous little objects, however sweet

Pattern

Be wary with pattern in small spaces. Usually when an area feels too congested or too small, pattern is best avoided especially on large surfaces. It is possible of course to make a statement with one large striking pattern but this needs the utmost care and flair

Placement

Place items such as furniture, pictures, lighting etc. so the eye can travel on

Shapes

Emphasise strong, straight, contemporary shapes (and fewer of them)

Space

With the 'nothing touching rule' you can impart an iconic quality to the most mundane objects:

- The centres of rooms kept empty

- Space behind, between and around everything, from the largest to the smallest. Have at least a finger's width around even the smallest item

- All items that impede or block easy passage through the space repositioned or eliminated

- Open plan. Sometimes it is possible to change the layout to 'magnify' the space. Walls can be knocked down for fewer, larger, free-flowing rooms. Going open plan or semi-open plan can make a previously poky house feel quite substantial with the twin delights of a sense of space and daylight from multiple directions

Note

The knocking down of walls to create a larger or open plan space needs to be very carefully thought out as you can easily find yourself with badly proportioned rooms. Knocking a front and back room into one, for example, is often unsatisfactory. The result can be a place where you can't quite settle, a long narrow corridor of a room with a big window at one end directly opposite a big window at the other and a 'dead' area in the middle. It is hard to relax there. In such rooms, the introduction of the golden mean 5:8 proportion in the furnishings and/ or décor can work wonders.

Squares

Squares make a space feel larger, for instance:

- ❧ Squares (e.g. square tiles) spanning corners of walls help blur the angles, making a small room 'bigger'
- ❧ Squares on floors, for example square floor tiles or square-patterned carpets and rugs
- ❧ Larger squares are more space-expanding than smaller squares

Staircases

Consider an open staircase since these 'expand' the whole space

Storage

One of the keys to space management is planned, flexible and creative storage. If you have a room you can spare, let the whole area be given over to storage so your other living spaces are free of major storage units. A bedroom without built-in or excess freestanding furniture can be very restful and agreeable

Surfaces

🍂 Gently reflective

🍂 Free of bits and pieces

Walls

The more wall and floor space visible the larger the space feels, so aim for walls as free as possible of visually distracting objects, especially at eye level. Aim for:

🍂 White or pale colours with a soft sheen (maybe with an odd dark or coloured wall to add interest and life)

🍂 Similar treatment of walls throughout interconnecting spaces

🍂 Smooth. Bumpy surfaces (woodchip, some wallpapers etc.) are to be avoided since they kill light

🍂 Uncluttered

🍂 One large original painting instead of lots of little prints

🍂 Favourite smaller paintings grouped together on one wall, leaving the walls as a whole clear and giving the dramatic effect of one large painting against a lot of empty wall. The group can be planned out first on the floor. Fitting the pictures into an overall golden mean can work well

❧ Walls kept empty (which, when sensitively plastered with softened corners, are beautiful in themselves). With modern technology, images (pictures, clocks, film etc.) can be projected onto plain walls as and when required

❧ If kitchen wall storage is absolutely necessary, open shelves are preferable as they give a greater feeling of space than closed units

❧ Underfloor central heating (which avoids wall-hung radiators). A bonus is that it can be more economical and eco-friendly

❧ Ceilings enlisted, for example with ceiling mounted speakers, to help keep walls clear

❧ Sound insulation

Note

Eye level is considered to be around 5ft–5ft 6in (152cm–168cm) but to suit the individual. Eye level is where we best see (and tend to look at) things. Use it only to your advantage. Place the things you want to look at, at eye level and never the things you don't. If hanging a group of pictures you can place the centre of the group at eye level.

X–factor – The Senses – Scent and Sound

❧ The aroma of green apples and cucumber. (*Bibliography: Hirsch*)

🌿 Flowers and plants

🌿 Energetic lively music with a strong beat

🌿 Sound insulation

Yin and Yang

Whilst a combination of yin and yang is vital, one key to making a room feel lighter and more spacious is to reduce the yin and/or increase the yang

The house or room that was dark and poky will now amaze you (and your friends). You have created space out of no space. You have become a shapeshifter of space.

Note

Occasionally any attempt to make a room feel light and bright may be doomed, especially where there is only a single north facing window. Then there is only one thing to do and that is to honour the darkness with strong, warm colour. Make it cosy. Celebrate what you have.

To Make a Space Feel Cosier and More Intimate

For the too-yang rooms, the too-bland rooms, the large stark unfriendly rooms, the rooms that incite burnout – for these rooms, something has to be done. Warmth, welcome and comfort need to be introduced. Again we can trick the eye.

Ceilings

- ❦ Warm, deep, strong advancing colour (even down to picture rail level)
- ❦ Matt surface

Colour

Aim for warm shades throughout the space

Fabrics

Soft fabrics, for example:

- ❦ Throws
- ❦ Cushions
- ❦ Tablecloths
- ❦ Curtains

Finishes

Let finishes be matt rather than reflective

Floors

- ❦ Carpets
- ❦ Thick rugs in strong or dark colour or richly patterned or with a long fleecy pile
- ❦ Dark flooring

Furniture

- 🐿 Low and long; e.g. an old bench instead of individual dining chairs
- 🐿 Dark antique furniture
- 🐿 Wooden furniture painted in vibrant colours
- 🐿 Padded cushions on chair seats
- 🐿 Squishy-squashy upholstery

Lighting

- 🐿 Warm
- 🐿 Down lighting from individual lamps to form pools of light (though it's best to avoid harsh ceiling down lighters as sole source of illumination)
- 🐿 Soft (you can use dimmer switches, lamplight, candlelight)
- 🐿 Table lamps
- 🐿 Accent lighting which creates shadows. (Shadows are always important but especially in the case of the too-large room with no personality)

Note

Avoid corner lighting as it 'expands' space

Lines

❧ Horizontal

❧ Curving

Lingam stones

Place a large lingam stone in any 'too-spacey' area to ground the energy

Paintwork

Use matt paints

Pattern

Pattern can help break up the starkness

Shapes

Indulge in curving or rounded shapes, for example oval tables and round cushions

Space

Large rooms can be zoned or partially divided, providing sitting, dining, office, television areas and so on, according to the room and your life. Semi-separate, more intimate spaces can be suggested with, for example:

❧ Colour

❧ Differing floor levels and ceiling heights

❧ Furnishings

❧ Screens or curtaining

❧ Shelving

❧ Partial-length walls

❧ Partial-height walls

Surfaces

Let surfaces be matt

Windows

❧ Smaller windows, especially multi-aspect

❧ Large windows subdivided into smaller panes (but sympathetic to the style/period of the house and to the wider environment)

Windows and the problem of glare

Normally we want to maximise light from our windows but with glare, as for instance from huge picture windows, we need to screen, filter and diffuse it. Everything possible needs to be done to avoid bouncing the harsh light around the room. Screening is one way and can be achieved with, for example:

❧ Light curtaining

❧ Blinds

- Stained glass

- Opaque glass

- Window film

- Trees or shrubs outside. (Soft light foliage that flutters in the breeze around windows is especially magical for its flickering shadows in the room)

- Fresh flowers, fruit, candles etc. on windowsills are best in opaque (not glass or reflective) containers

Window reveals

Matt and/or textured to absorb the light. Any texturing needs to be extremely subtle, preferably using soft lime or clay plaster

X-factor – The senses – Scent and Sound

- A fire (or in summer, fireplace/stove made to speak of warmth in some other way)

- Candles

- Peaceful, serene, calming music

- Flowers and plants soften space

- Lavender and roses and the scent of lavender and roses. (*Bibliography*: *Hirsch*)

Yin and Yang

Excess yang reduced and/or yin increased

To 'Change the Shape' of a Room

Some rooms just feel 'wrong'. For example a room may be too long and narrow in which case we need to make a long side wall seem farther away and/or a short end wall feel closer. Or, perhaps a hall seems too wide and uncontained in which case we might 'bring a wall in'. By means such as the deliberate use of advancing or receding colour we can transform apparent shape and proportion.

To make a wall feel further away

- The wall painted/decorated white or in a receding colour

- Wall surface gently reflective

- Wall well lit

- A large mirror (or a 'painting with depth') hung on the wall

- Floorboards (or stripes on rugs or carpets) running towards the wall. With floorboards the effect is emphasised if the boards are painted (making the joints more visible)

- Floor tiles laid brick-fashion, the main grouting lines running towards the wall

- Rectangular rugs, coffee tables etc. running towards the wall (short end to the wall)

- Wall-hugging furniture is best on legs or 'floating', so you can see underneath to the wall behind

To make a wall feel closer

- The wall painted/decorated in an advancing colour. White woodwork or splashes of colour may counteract any feeling of heaviness

- Matt wall surface

- Specific lighting of the wall avoided

- A big comfy sofa or a large cupboard etc. placed against the wall can reduce the distance physically

- Wall-hugging storage furniture solid to the floor (blocking the view of the floor below and wall behind)

- A long narrow space can be broken up with furniture, rugs, screening, art, artefacts, plants and the like (but beware of over furnishing)

To make a small space seem longer

We perceive things close by as larger, brighter, more strongly coloured and wider apart. Things further away look smaller, paler and closer together and lines seem to converge. To give a greater feeling of distance we can work with this illusion. Perspective can be suggested by:

- Large items slanted almost imperceptibly in towards an imaginary distant 'vanishing point'. For example two sofas which face each other lengthways along the room can be slanted so as to converge ever so slightly towards the far end of the room

- Smaller, lower items and those of a more receding colour placed at the far end

- Eye-catching items placed at the far end of the room – even beyond (through a window into the garden if that is possible) to lead the eye on

- 'Views beyond', for example a garden glimpsed through a French window

- Colour more receding towards the far end of the space

- Floor tiles laid on the diagonal

To make a long space seem shorter

The far wall

- Painted/decorated in an advancing colour

- Having a matt surface

- Unlit

When a room is too long and narrow

- On the short end walls: strong advancing colour

- On the long side walls: white or a pale receding colour. Large mirrors can help give the illusion of greater width, especially when placed opposite a doorway

When a room *really* is too long and narrow

Creative solutions paying homage to the space-as-it-is are often the best way forward as for example, turning the whole into an 'art gallery' complete with track lighting

To make a room feel higher

Ceiling

🕊 White or a pale receding colour

🕊 Slightly reflective (with a soft sheen)

🕊 Smooth – no swirls or bumps which eat light

🕊 Up-lighted

🕊 Beams avoided if possible, otherwise lime-washed white or the same shade as the ceiling

Walls

🕊 Wall colour paler towards the top of the walls

🕊 Space between shelves graded, from deeper at the bottom to shallower at the top

🕊 On shelves; the larger, taller items placed lower and the smaller, shorter items higher

🕊 Verticals favoured over horizontals, as for example with full length curtains or tall sculpture, wall hangings, plants or furniture (though regular verticals as in vertical stripes usually best avoided)

To make a space feel lower

Ceiling

🕊 Advancing colour (including the area above the picture rail)

🐾 Matt ceiling surface

🐾 Pendant lighting (if present) low hanging

Walls

🐾 Panelling on the lower part of the walls

🐾 Horizontals emphasised, for instance with picture rails, dados, partial-height panelling, deep skirting boards

🐾 Architectural features (such as the tops of doors) and decorative features (e.g. the tops of pictures) forming a single horizontal 'line'

To balance a sloping ceiling

Sloping ceilings can feel uncomfortable but the following can help:

Around the whole room

A horizontal line (actual or suggested) created right around the room

On the low wall

🐾 Verticals: for example a tall mirror or tall plants

🐾 Up lighters (can help 'lift' the low ceiling)

On the high wall

🎋 Horizontals

🎋 Down lighters from individual lamps, low-hung pendants to form pools of light, low-slung spotlights with beam directed low

A total rethink

The quirkiness celebrated rather than camouflaged

To 'widen' a staircase

🎋 A large mirror on the staircase wall

🎋 White/very pale staircase wall

🎋 Stair carpet with horizontal stripes (not stripes running vertically up the staircase)

🎋 Replacement of enclosing wall with banisters

To help a staircase feel less steep

Emphasise the horizontal and reduce any sense of downward pull with, for example:

🎋 Painted horizontal borders

🎋 The tops of pictures on the same horizontal level (not sloping down)

🦋 Art evoking lightness, buoyancy and upward mobility

Notes

1. Sometimes these suggestions clash, inevitably. Use one or the other to suit you.

2. You don't have to use every one (or even any) of these tricks, everywhere, every time. Keep it simple.

3. You must like the measures you take.

Bibliography

References &
Resources

Feng shui, Clutter clearing, Space clearing

Collins, Terah Kathryn. (1996). *The Western Guide to Feng Shui: Creating balance, harmony and prosperity in your environment.* Hay House.

Collins, Terah Kathryn. (1999). *Home Design 9 with Feng Shui A-Z.* Hay House.

Collins, Terah Kathryn. (1999). *The Western Guide to Feng Shui Room by Room.* Hay House.

Collins, Terah Kathryn. (2004). *The Western Guide to Feng Shui for Romance: The dance of heart and home.* Hay House.

Collins, Terah Kathryn. (2008). *The Western Guide to Feng Shui for Prosperity: True accounts of people who have applied Essential Feng Shui to their lives and prospered.* Revised ed. Hay House.

Howe Elkins, Valmai. (1999). *Adventures of a Feng Shui Detective: How outer clues reveal your inner life.* Montreal: Woodley & Watts.

Kingston, Karen. (1996). *Creating Sacred Space with Feng Shui.* London: Piatkus.

Kingston, Karen. (2016). *Clear Your Clutter with Feng Shui.* 3rd ed. New York.

Lambert, Mary. (2013). Living with Less: *How to downsize to 100 personal possessions.* Cico Books.

Lazenby, Gina. (2000). *The Healthy Home.* London: Conran Octopus Limited.

Linn, Denise. (1999). *Altars: Bringing sacred shrines into your everyday life.* London: Rider.

Linn, Denise. (2000). *Space Clearing: How to purify and create harmony in your home.* London: Ebury Press.

Linn, Denise. (2001). Space clearing A-Z: *How to use feng shui to purify and bless your home.* Hay House.

Linn, Denise. (2009). *Feng Shui for the Soul: How to create a harmonious environment that will nurture and sustain you.* Random House.

Linn, Denise. (2010). *Sacred Space: Clearing and enhancing the energy of your home and office.* Random House.

Architecture

Alexander, Christopher. (1977). *A Pattern Language: Towns. Buildings. Construction.* New York: Oxford University Press.

Alexander, Christopher. (1979). *The Timeless Way of Building. New York:* Oxford University Press.

Bangs, Herbert. (2006). *The Return of Sacred Architecture: The golden ratio and the end of modernism. Vermont: Inner Traditions Bear and Company.*

Day, Christopher. (1990). *Building with Heart.* Green Books.

Day, Christopher. (1998). *A Haven for Childhood.* Starborn Books.

Day, Christopher. (2002). *Spirit & Place.* Oxford: Architectural Press.

Day, Christopher. (2003). *Consensus Design: Socially inclusive process.* Oxford: Architectural Press.

Day, Christopher. (2007). *Environment and Children.* Oxford: Architectural Press.

Day, Christopher. (2014). *Places of the Soul.* Routledge.

Day, Christopher. (2015). *The Eco-Home Design Guide.* Green Books.

De Botton, Alain. (2006). *The Architecture of Happiness: The Secret of Art of Furnishing Your Life.* London: *Penguin.*

Frederick, Matthew. (2007). *101 Things I Learned in Architecture School.* 3rd ed. Cambridge, Massachusetts: MIT Press.

Hale, Jonathan. (1995). *The Old Way of Seeing: How architecture lost its magic and how to get it back.* Boston/New York: Houghton Mifflin Company.

Kellert, Stephen R. Heerwagen, Judith. and Mador, Martin. (2008). *Biophilic Design: The Theory, Science and Practice of Bringing Buildings to Life.* Wiley.

Lawlor, Anthony. (1995). *The Temple in the House: Finding the sacred in everyday architecture.* New York: Jeremy P. Tarcher.

Lawlor, Anthony. (1997). *A Home for the Soul: A guide for dwelling with spirit and imagination.* Clarkson Potter.

Design

Goodman, Chris. (2011). *Lifetime Homes Design Guide*. IHS BRE Press.

Kellert, Stephen R. Heerwagen, Judith. and Mador, Martin. (2008). *Biophilic Design: The Theory, Science and Practice of Bringing Buildings to Life*. Wiley.

Lidwell, William. Holden, Kritina. and Butler, Jill. (2010). *Universal Principles of Design*. Beverly, Massachusetts: Rockport Publishers. Inc. (Quayside Publishing).

WEBSITES:

www.homebuilding.co.uk/design/design-guides/design-style
www.woodheat.org (for fireplace/chimney design)

Eco–architecture, eco–building, healthy homes

Day, Christopher. (2015). *The Eco-Home Design Guide*. Green Books.

Hall, Keith. (Ed). *The Green Building Bible*. (Handbook). Green Building Press.

Lazenby, Gina. (2000). *The Healthy Home*. London: Conran Octopus Limited.

WEBSITES:

www.cat.org.uk
www.greenbuildingpress.co.uk
www.newbuilder.co.uk
www.thehealthyhome.com
www.womersleys.co.uk
https://en.wikipedia.org/wiki/Bosco_Verticale

Fractal architecture

Batty, Michael. and Longley, Paul. (1994). *Fractal Cities: A geometry of form and function*. London: Academic Press Limited.

Batty, M. and Xie, Y. (1996). Preliminary Evidence for a
    Theory of the Fractal City. *Environment and Planning*. Vol.
    28 pp. 1745-1762.
WEBSITES: Many websites, for example:
    http//zeta.math.utsa.edu/~yxk833/connecting.html

Fractals: The Mandelbrot Set

Lipton, Bruce. (2011). *The Biology of Belief*. UK: Hay House.

Fractals: Miscellaneous

Barnsley, Michael. (2012). *Fractals Everywhere*. Reissue. Dover
    Publications.
Braden, Gregg. (2010). *Fractal Time: The secret of 2012 and a new
    world age*. Carlsbad/London: Hay House.
Dossey MD, Larry. (2013). *One Mind: How our individual mind Is
    part of a greater consciousness and why it matters*. London. Hay
    House Ltd.
Crilly, A.J. Earnshaw, Rae. and Jones, Huw. (eds). (2011).
    Fractals and Chaos. London: Springer.
Lipton, Bruce. (2011). *The Biology of Belief*. UK: Hay House.
Mandelbrot, Benoit B. (1982). *The Fractal Geometry of Nature*.
    Revised ed. W H Freeman and Co. Ltd.
WEBSITES: Many, for example:
    http://homepages.uel.ac.uk/1953r/fracexa.htm
    Or: Google 'Fractals', 'Fractals in nature', 'Fractals in
    architecture' etc.

Golden mean, Fibonacci sequence, sacred geometry

Bangs, Herbert. (2006). *The Return of Sacred Architecture: The golden ratio and the end of modernism.* Vermont: Inner Traditions Bear and Company.

Braden, Gregg. (2010). *Fractal Time: The secret of 2012 and a new world age.* Carlsbad/London: Hay House.

Corbalan, Fernando. (2012). *The Golden Ratio: The beautiful language of mathematics.* Rba Coleccionables.

Schneider, Michael S. (2003). *A Beginner's Guide to Constructing the Universe: The mathematical archetypes of nature, art and science.* Avon Books.

WEBSITES: Numerous, for example: *www.enc.org/features/calen¬dar/unit/0,1819,152,00.shtm* (This website gives other links).

Or, Google 'Golden mean', 'Golden mean in nature', 'Golden mean in architecture' etc.

Gardens and gardening

Bartholomew, Mel. (2013). *Square Metre Gardening.* Frances Lincoln.

Dunford, Chauney. (2013). *Grow All You Can Eat in Three Square Feet.* DK.

Maguire, Kay. with the RHS. (2013). *Grow Your Own Crops In Pots.* London: Mitchell Beazley.

Swift, Katherine. (2009). *The Morville Hours.* London: Bloomsbury Publishing PLC.

WEBSITES: Many relevant websites. Here are a few:
Biodynamic gardening   *www.biodynamic.org.uk*
Dew ponds   *http://dewponds.co.uk*

	www.countrylife.co.uk/dew-ponds-to-therescue-36183
Grey water systems	http://greywateraction.org/contentabout-greywater-reuse
Organic gardening	www.soilassociation.org
Permaculture	www.permaculture.org.uk
Porous landscaping	www.landscapingnetwork.com/paving/permeable.html
Rain gardens	http://raingardens.info
Everything!	www.cat.org.uk

Harmony

HRH The Prince of Wales. Juniper, Tony. and Skelly, Ian. (2010). *Harmony: A new way of looking at our world.* London: Blue Door, an imprint of HarperCollins Publishers.

Light: wellbeing & environment

Hobday, Richard. (2007). *The Light Revolution: Health, architecture and the sun.* UK:. Findhorn Press.

Lighting: 'blue-rich' LEDs – potential harmful effects

WEBSITES: Many websites, for example:
https://wiki.physics.udel.edu/AAP/Blue_light_and_sleep_deprivation
www.bbc.co.uk/news/health-30574260
www.earthisland.org
www.health.harvard.edu/newsletters/Harvard_Health_Letter/2012/May/blue-light-has-a-dark-side
www.nhs.uk/news/2013/05May/Pages/Do-iPads-and-electric-lights-disturb-sleep.aspx
www.upi.com/Science_News/2013/05/11/LED-lights-ruin-retinas

Lighting: hybrid solar

http://en.wikipedia.org/wiki/Hybrid_solar_lighting
www.brightenyourhome.net/Hybrid-Solar-Lighting.html
www.explainthatstuff.com/hybrid-solar-lighting.html

Lighting: star-friendly/environmentally friendly outdoor lighting

WEBSITES:

www.britastro.org/dark-skies
http://darksky.org/lighting/lighting-basics

Plants. Fresh air. Biophilia. Biophilic architecture

Drummond, Ian. and O'Reilly, Kara. (2017). At Home with
Plants. Octopus Publishing Group.

Kellert, Stephen R. Heerwagen, Judith. and Mador, Martin.
(2008). *Biophilic Design: The Theory, Science and Practice of
Bringing Buildings to Life.* Wiley.

Wilson, Edward O. (1990). *Biophilia.* Harvard University Press,
New Ed edition.

Wolverton, Dr B.C. (1997). *How to Grow Fresh Air: 50
Houseplants that Purify Your Home or Office.* Penguin

WEBSITES: Numerous, for example:

en.wikipedia.org/wiki/NASA_Clean_Air_Study
http://public.wsu.edu/~lohr/hih/productivity
www.biophilicdesign.net
www.dailymail.co.uk/health/article-106018/Pot-plant-power.html
*www.homesandproperty.co.uk/home-garden/gardening/clean-air-
save-your-home-from-harmful-pollution-with-clever-garden-hedge-
choices-a114961.html*

www.ncbi.nlm.nih.gov/pmc/articles/PMC3230460
www.wolvertonenvironmental.com/air.htm
www.workingwellresources.com/2009/11/18/indoor-plants-rated-as-top-indoor-air-cleaners-by-university-of-georgia
https://en.wikipedia.org/wiki/Bosco_Verticale
www.stefanoboeriarchitetti.net/en/project/vertical-forest

Sanctuary, house blessing

Doherty, Catherine. (2000). *Poustinia: Encountering God in silence, solitude and prayer.* 3rd ed. Canada: Madonna House Publications.

Frank, Ann Wall. (1996). *Bless This House: A collection of blessings to make a house your home.* Chicago: Contemporary Books.

For a traditional Christian house blessing see:

(1979). *The Book of Occasional Services.* New York: Church Hymnal Corporation.

Hershey, Terry. (2015). *Sanctuary: Creating a space for grace in your life.* Chicago: Loyola Press.

MacWeeney, Alen. and Ness, Caro. (2002). *A Space for Silence.* Frances Lincoln.

Reinhart, Melanie. (December 2015, monthly newsletter). *Solstice 2015 greetings from Melanie.*

WEBSITES:

http://progressivechristianity.org/events/creating-sanctuary-for-ourselves-and-others
www.melaniereinhart.com
www.signology.org
www.starwalkerpress.com
www.whats-your-sign.com

Symbolism in the home

Howe Elkins, Valmai. (1999). *Adventures of a Feng Shui Detective: How outer clues reveal your inner life*. Montreal: Woodley & Watts.

Research

Design

Anthes, Emily. (April 2009). How Room Designs Affect Your Work and Mood. *Scientific American Mind.*

Anthes, Emily. (May 2009). Building Around The Mind: Brain research can help us craft spaces that relax, inspire, awaken, comfort and heal. *Scientific American. Mind. Behavior, Brain Science, Insights.*

Bar, Moshe. and Neta, Maital. (2006). Humans Prefer Curved Visual Objects. *Psychological Science*. Volume 17.

Bar, Moshe. and Neta, Maital. (2007). Visual Elements of Subjective Preference Modulate Amygdala Activation. *Neuropsychologia*. Volume 45.

Meyers-Levy, Joan. and Rui Zhu, Juliet. (August 2007).The Influence of Ceiling Height: The effect of priming on the type of processing that people use. *Journal of Consumer Research*. Volume 34.

Environmental over-stimulation

Baniel, Anat. (December 2013). The Science of Subtlety. *What Doctors Don't Tell You.*

Fisher, Anna V. Godwin, Karrie E. and Seltman, Howard.
    (Carnegie Mellon University, Pittsburgh. Pennsylania).
    (September 2014). Heavily Decorated Classrooms Disrupt
    Attention and Learning in Young Children. *News article of
    the Association for Psychological Science.*

McMains, Stephanie. and Kastner, Sabine. (January 2011).
    Interactions of Top-Down and Bottom-Up Mechanisms in
    Human Visual Cortex. *The Journal of Neuroscience.*

WEBSITES:
    There are many website scholarly articles on the
    implications of over stimulation. See for example: Weber's
    Law (Weber-Fechner Law).

Fire

Lynn, Christopher. (November 2014). Hearth and campfire
    influences on arterial blood pressure: defraying the costs
    of the social brain through fireside relaxation. *Journal of
    Evolutionary Psychology.*

WEBSITES:
    *www.glowing-embers.co.uk/blog/are-wood-burning-stoves-eco-
    friendly*
    www.woodheat.org/wood-burning-and-the-environment.html

Music

Research on the ability of music to reduce blood pressure:
    Sleight, Peter. (2015). Emeritus Fellow in Cardiovascular
    Medicine, University of Exeter.

WEBSITE:

www.exeter.ox.ac.uk/node/1793

For a popular book by a serious researcher, see also:

Langer, Ellen. (2010). *Counterclockwise.* London: Hodder & Stoughton Ltd.

Scent

Moss, Mark. Cook, J. Wesnes, K. and Duckett. P. (January 2003). Aromas of rosemary and lavender essential oils differentially affect cognition and mood in healthy adults *International Journal of Neuroscience.*

Moss et al. (many subsequent studies on rosemary and memory, for example:

Moss, Mark. and McCready, Jemma. (April 2013). Rosemary aroma may help you remember to do things. *Annual conference paper for the British Psychogical Society.*

For a popular book by a serious researcher, see also:

Hirsch, Dr Alan J. (2003). *Life's a Smelling Success: Using scent to empower your memory and learning.* Authors of Unity Publishing

WEBSITES:

http://themindunleashed.org/2014/07/scientists-find-sniffing-rosemary-can-increase-memory-75.html

www.smellandtaste.org, (Research & treatment organisation of neurologist Dr Alan J. Hirsch).

Miscellaneous

Fire: mythology

Anderson, Flavia. (1988). *The Ancient Secret: Fire from the Sun.* Research into Lost Knowledge Organisation Trust.

Monaghan, Patricia. (1997). *The New Book of Goddesses & Heroines*. 3rd ed. Llewellyn Publications.

ENCYCLOPAEDIAS:

Jordan, Michael. *Encyclopedia of Gods*. Kyle Cathie Ltd.

Larousse. *World Mythology*.

The Hutchinson *Unabridged Encyclopaedia*.

Firewood

Thomson, Andy. (2006). *Native British Trees*. New York: Wooden Books Ltd.

Interior design

Burdon, Jane. (2005). *Room Rescues: Decorating solutions for awkward spaces*. London: Ryland Peters and Small.

Llewelyn-Bowen, Laurence. (2003). *Design Rules*. London: Contender Books.

Wilson, Judith. (2008). *Harmonious Home*. London: Ryland Peters and Small.

Labyrinths

Artress, Lauren. (2006). *Walking a Sacred Path: Rediscovering the labyrinth as a sacred tool*. Revised ed. New York: Riverhead Books.

Lonegren, Sig. (2007). *Labyrinths: Ancient myths and modern uses*. 4th ed. Gothic Image.

Sayward, Jeff. (2003). *Labyrinths & Mazes*. Gaia Press.

Sayward, Jeff. (2008). *Labyrinths & Mazes in the 21st century*. London: Mitchell Beazley

Williams, Di. (2011). *Labyrinth: Landscape of the Soul.* Wild Goose.
WEBSITES:

>   *www.diwilliams.com*
>   *www.labyrinthos.net*
>   *www.labyrinthsociety,org*
>   *www.veriditas.org*

Moon calendars & diaries

WEBSITES:

>   *www.edgeoftime.co.uk*
>   *www.the-gardeners-calendar.co.uk/moon_planting.asp*

Muscle tests: validation

WEBSITES:

>   *www.holisticdental.org/muscletestcomparison.html*

Piezoelectricity

Church, Dawson. (2014). *The Genie In Your Genes.* Energy
    Psychology Press.
WEBITES:

>   Numerous

Quiet Garden Movement

WEBSITES:

>   *www.quietgarden.org*

Other sources & resources

The British Library, radio and television, the internet, jour-
nals & magazines, conversations, friends, places, spaces, life.

Note

Check also: e-books, audio books, articles, videos, films, blogs etc. for the above authors.

Quotations

"A fractal is basically the iterations of an equation forever, the unique thing about them is that they are equally complex at any magnification. If you took a fractal and magnified it by 500x, you would see the same level of detail as you did on the entire thing. Fractals are among the most beautiful of all mathematical forms." Mandelbrot, Benoit. (Polish-born mathematician, 1924- 2010). Interview.
See: *www.3villagecsd.k12.ny.us/wmhs/Departments/Math/OBrien/mandlebrot.html*

"Fractals are the unique, irregular patterns left behind by the unpredictable movements of the chaotic world at work." Kluge, Tino. et al. (December 2005). Abstract: Fractals and Dynamic Systems: Fractals in nature and applications. (University of Wales, Aberystwyth: Language and Learning Centre). See: *kluge.in-chemnitz.de/documents/fractal/node2.html*

The golden mean: "… is a scale of proportions which makes the bad difficult (to produce) and the good easy". Einstein, Albert. (1879 -1955). Letter to the architect Le Corbusier. (1887-1965).

"Have nothing in your house that …" i.e. from "If you want a golden rule that will fit everything, this is it: Have nothing in your houses that you do not know to be useful or believe to be beautiful." William Morris. (1834-1896). I cannot find the original source of this much-quoted maxim. If you know it, please let the author know. Thank you.

"Less is more". Browning, Robert. (1812-1899). (Poem: Andrea del Sarto). Later popularised by architect Mies van der Rohe, Ludvig. (1886–1969), a founding father of the Bauhaus School of Architecture and, together with Walter Gropius and Le Corbusier, one of the pioneers of twentieth century architecture.

"Mirror mirror on the wall, who is the fairest of them all?" The Brothers Grimm. (1812, final revision 1854). Snow White. Grimm's Fairy Tales. Tale 53. (In the 1937 Disney film version Snow White and the Seven Dwarfs this is quoted as "Magic mirror on the wall, who is the fairest one of all?").

"There's rosemary, that's for remembrance, pray love, remember; and there is pansies, that's for thoughts." Shakespeare, William. (1564-1616). Hamlet, Act 4, Scene 5. Ophelia's speech.

"When you sleep in a house your thoughts are as high as the ceiling, when you sleep outside they are as high as the stars."(Bedouin saying)
See: *proverbicals.com/bedouin-proverbs*

And Now...

An Irish Blessing

God bless the corners of this house,
And be the lintel blest,
And bless the hearth and bless the board,
And bless each place of rest,
And bless each door that opens wide
To stranger as to kin,
And bless each crystal window pane
That lets the starlight in,
And bless the rooftree overhead
And every sturdy wall.
The peace of man, the peace of God,
The peace of love on all.

—*Anonymous*